Maps Mean Adventure

MAPS MEAN

OTHER BOOKS BY CHRISTIE McFALL

OUR COUNTRY AMERICA

A BOOK ABOUT HAWAII

ADVENTURE

Written and illustrated by

CHRISTIE McFALL

DODD, MEAD & COMPANY

NEW YORK

To Grace and Minor McChristie who at age
seven and ten ambitiously attempted to map
Colorado Springs—on bicycles.

The author wishes to express his appreciation to
Betsy Durfee and Olga McFall for their assistance
in the preparation of this book.

Contents

1.   The World at Your Fingertips

Map-making is an exciting adventure. In the "Age of Discovery," when many new parts of the world were being explored, map-making, or cartography, became one of the foremost professions. Many explorers such as Columbus, Champlain and Cook were also cartographers skilled in the art of drawing maps and charts.

Gathering the knowledge to make accurate maps was difficult. There were few instruments with which to obtain information. Explorers sought to discover the size and shape of the lands they explored, and noted such things as rivers which might afford a passageway through a new continent, or the position of native villages or waterfalls. Maps opened the way to trade and settlement of these new lands.

10

Today we are in a new age of discovery and adventure, and map-makers—cartographers—are busy keeping pace with man's new knowledge. The ocean depths are being mapped with increasing accuracy and speed. Weather satellites give data for new and better maps of the atmosphere. Man's adventures in space will bring new kinds of maps. The first detailed map of the moon is nearly complete and will show its many mountains and craters. Photographs taken from cartographic satellites may soon give us our first completely accurate map of the world!

In the first Age of Discovery, maps were precious, expensive and often kept under lock and key. Thousands of different maps are available today. Many maps can be purchased for a small sum or are even given away free. Several hundred million maps are printed and made available each year — not counting those in atlases, text books, or the weather maps in the daily newspapers.

The National Geographic Society prints and distributes twelve million maps a year to its members. The Geological Survey prints four million topographic maps in a year. Enough road maps are produced each year to give one to every man, woman and child in the United States.

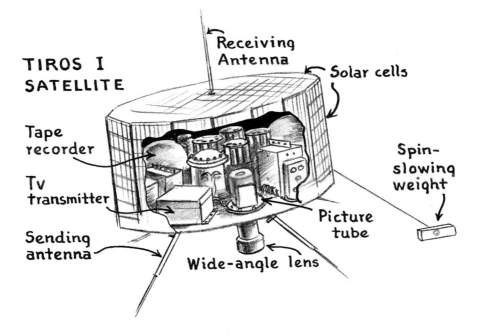

TIROS I SATELLITE

Receiving Antenna

Solar cells

Tape recorder

Tv transmitter

Sending antenna

Wide-angle lens

Picture tube

Spin-slowing weight

During World War II troops landing on the North African coast in November of 1942 took with them 110 tons of military maps. Within three months, 400 more tons arrived — over 10 million maps in all.

The variety of maps in existence today is almost as overwhelming as the number of maps produced and used. No longer are cartographers concerned only with maps that show land masses and bodies of water. There are weather maps, road maps, charts of waterways and coastal regions, maps of the stars and heavenly bodies, airline routes, maps showing the positions of radio facilities, and tidal charts, to name only a portion. These may be *topographic* maps in which elevations of the same height are connected by lines called *contour lines*. They may be *relief* maps which show by a raised surface the physical features of the place mapped. They may be *Mercator* maps which use parallel longitude lines and latitude lines. Learning to read and use all these kinds of maps is a fascinating adventure.

Yet with all these maps and charts, there is still a great need for more and better map-making. As man's horizons expand — from ocean bottoms to outer space — cartographers must add new knowledge to existing maps, make changes as areas are explored more thoroughly, chart regions that have never been ventured into before. In an age of rockets and missiles, there is a need to know the exact shape of the earth and precise distances between points on the earth. Directing missiles over a 5,000 to 9,000 mile course demands pinpoint accuracy in determining distances. Satellites are helping to determine these exact measurements. Vanguard I, the first United States satellite, proved so regular and its orbit was charted so accurately that points on Wake, Guam and other oceanic islands were found to be nearly a mile out of position from previous plottings.

Tiros I, the weather satellite launched in early 1960, was the first to photograph the earth with television cameras. Al-

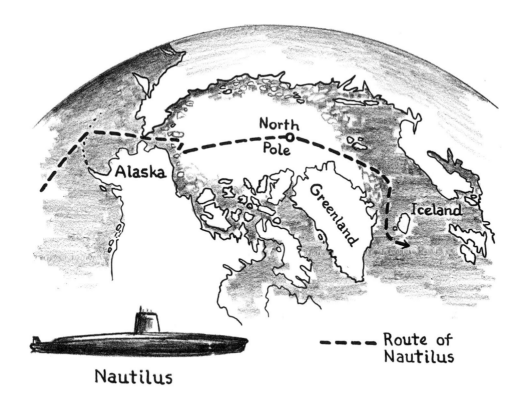

North Pole

Alaska

Greenland

Iceland

Nautilus

- - - - Route of Nautilus

though its purpose was weather detection, it is a forerunner of cartographic satellites. These Samos satellites, whirling about the earth above the poles, will be able to observe and photograph the earth from a height of 100 to 400 miles. Photographs will be sharp enough so that accurate detailed maps may be made from them.

Mapping the seas and the surfaces beneath them is gaining importance, too. In 1958, the United States atomic submarine *Nautilus* traveled 1,830 miles under the polar ice pack. During the voyage, the crew made continuous measurements of both the depth of the sea and the thickness of the ice, expanding man's knowledge of the Arctic region. Men temporarily stationed on large ice islands in that icy area also carry out scientific projects — measuring the depth of the water and

13

obtaining a good picture of the ocean floor. Ocean currents are also studied and new, more accurate maps are made.

A map is seldom complete. As new knowledge is obtained, maps must be corrected. A recent National Geographic map of South America, made with aerial photographs, locates two rivers as much as sixty miles from their previously charted positions. Even if new information was not constantly being made available, the world itself changes and maps must change to keep up with it. Some of this change is slow. Mountains wear down, valleys are cut deeper and rivers change their channels. Islands become peninsulas, new bays appear, shorelines recede or expand. The Mississippi River has changed so much over the years that nearly all of the river that La Salle floated down in 1682 is now dry land. Old channels fill with silt and new ones branch out. Map models have been made to study the flow of the Mississippi and its tributaries.

The pounding sea wears away at our coastline in one place, and deposits sand and debris in another. In the last half century, over 5,500 acres of New Jersey beachfront have been worn away by the waves, but at the same time 3,000 acres have been deposited at other places along the shore. The point of Sandy Hook continues to add 100 feet to its length each year. Water plunging over Niagara Falls constantly deepens and widens the pool at its base. From time to time the cap rock breaks off and the falls move gradually upstream. The Canadian Falls has been traveling upstream at a rate of 2.3 feet a year.

Sometimes nature moves with speed, however. In August, 1959, the earth shook and the top of a 7,600-foot mountain tore loose and spilled down into the Madison River near Yellowstone Park. The earthquake left a barrier of debris 300 feet high. It dried up the river downstream and created Earthquake Lake behind the new dam. Overnight, maps of the area were obsolete. Scientists and engineers moved in to make new surveys; cartographers made new maps.

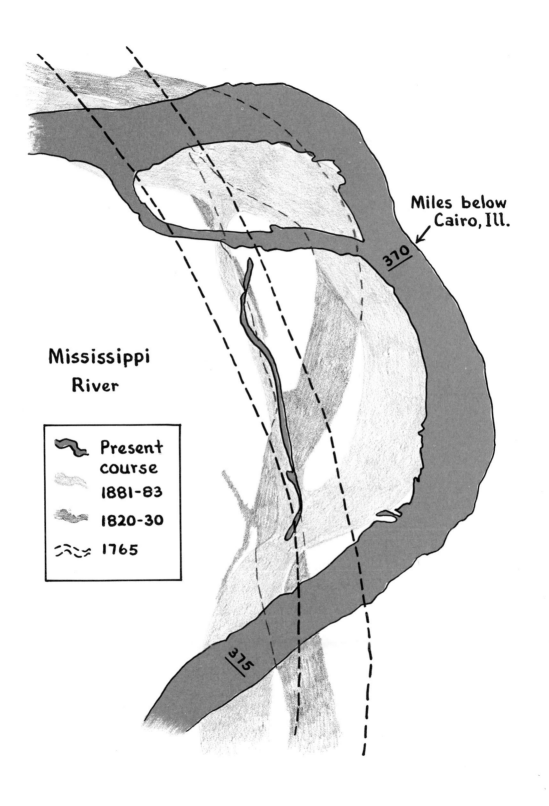

Miles below
Cairo, Ill.

370

Mississippi
River

Present course	
1881-83	
1820-30	
1765	

375

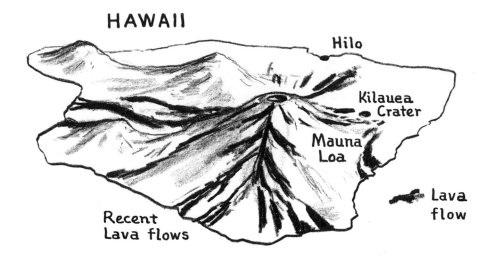

HAWAII

Hilo

Kilauea Crater

Mauna Loa

Lava flow

Recent Lava flows

Sixteen years earlier, in a cornfield near the village of Parícutin, Mexico, rose a 1,500-foot volcano spouting lava and steam. A new mountain had to be added to the maps. In 1883, Krakatoa, an island volcano, exploded. In minutes it destroyed its cone and its island foundation to 1,000 feet below sea level. A mountain had to be subtracted. Our new state of Hawaii was built by volcanoes and is still growing. Eruptions occur every few years, pouring glowing rivers of lava across the island. More land is added to the fiftieth state.

Man is also at work changing the face of the earth. He dredges harbors to provide new waterways, cuts down hills and tunnels through mountains to build new highways. He dams rivers, forms new lakes and reservoirs and cuts canals. Much of New York City rests on filled-in land, part of it dredged up out of the harbor. Both LaGuardia and Idlewild International airports in New York are built on reclaimed land. Maps must be redrawn in order to be up-to-date.

Across the Atlantic, the Dutch are hard at work pumping dry the Zuider Zee. A twenty-mile dike across its mouth walls

16

out the ocean which is twenty feet higher than the rich farm
land that will be added to Holland. The Zuider Zee will dis-
appear from maps. In our western states, our largest reservoir
is a man-made lake — Lake Mead, formed when Hoover Dam
was built. It covers 227 square miles of former waste lands. In
the East, the huge TVA has converted the Tennessee Valley
into an area with 10,000 miles of shoreline. Each new lake, each
change, must find its place on the latest maps of the region.

New towns and cities appear on maps and old ones disap-
pear. Virginia City, Nevada, was settled in 1859 and for many
years yielded one-half the silver mined in the United States.
It and many other colorful towns, such as Bumble Bee, Ari-
zona, are now ghost towns and have long since disappeared
from our maps. But new towns and cities are springing up

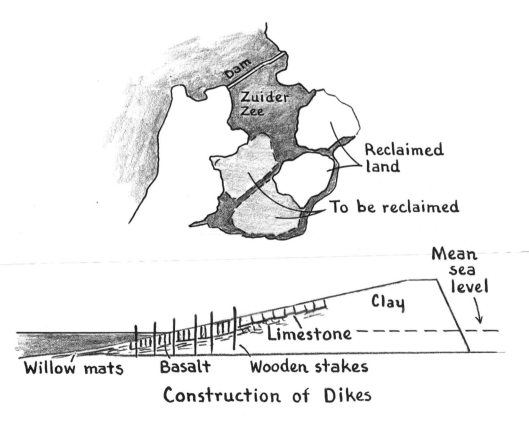

Construction of Dikes

across our nation. Levittown, Long Island, rose out of potato fields to become in a few years a city of 70,000 population. In Brazil the new modern capital, Brazilia, is being carved out of tropical forests.

So you see, the map-maker — like the housewife — finds his work is never done. Fortunately, that work no longer need be done all by hand. With the aid of electronic computers for making calculations, and aerial photography, maps can be mass-produced and machines can do in a few weeks what would take one man 100 years to accomplish.

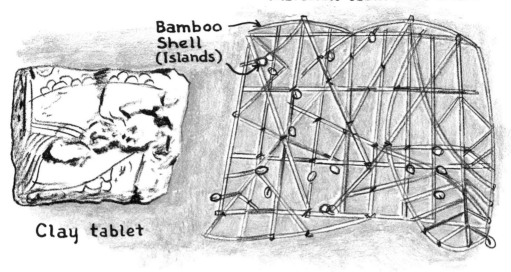

Marshall Islander's chart

Bamboo
Shell
(Islands)

Clay tablet

2.   Historic Maps and Voyages

Have you ever taken a stick and made a drawing or map in the dirt?

Making maps is an old, old means of expressing an idea. From the dawn of history men have made maps by tracing a line in sand or dirt. Babylonian land surveys were carved in clay tablets. Other maps have been made of bark or cut in stone.

The Greeks laid the foundation for our present system of cartography. They recognized the earth as a sphere which they roughly measured. They also developed longitude and latitude and the first map "projections." Most of our knowledge of the ancient world comes from Claudius Ptolemy of Alexandria. He created the first known atlas in 150 A. D. For thirteen centuries his world map was the most reliable map available.

In the latter part of the fifteenth century the printing press was developed and Ptolemy's "Geographia" was printed in large quantities. It became a foundation for atlases and maps during the Age of Discovery, when map and chart making became an important trade. The Flemish and Dutch became the foremost cartographers. Dutch maps were carefully drawn and skillfully engraved. Probably the most famous of the Flemish map-makers was Gerardus Mercator whose world projection is still the best known and one of the most useful.

New charts appeared almost yearly, adding to existing knowledge that of the new lands being discovered and explored. By the latter part of the fifteenth century, Portuguese expeditions had sailed far down the coast of Africa. They marked their new discoveries with stone columns.

But America remained blocked off by a mysterious ocean thought by many to be filled with sea serpents and other monsters. It bore the forbidding name "Sea of Darkness." On maps of Columbus' time this vast ocean spread out between western Europe and eastern Asia. It was nearly four centuries before the continents of North and South America took shape on maps as we know them today.

Columbus had studied map-making and navigation in Lisbon. However, only a small fragment of his work is preserved. A sketch of Hispaniola, the islands claimed for Spain in the New World by Columbus, marks the spot where his ship, the *Santa Maria*, struck a coral reef and had to be abandoned.

On Columbus' second voyage he was accompanied by Juan de la Cosa as official cartographer. La Cosa's parchment map of 1500 is the earliest known map to show any part of the western world.

Samuel de Champlain was one of the foremost map-maker explorers. Champlain served as royal geographer to the king of France. He recorded in a series of maps the results of his journeys and those under his command between 1603 and

1616. Champlain explored the coastline of North America from Cape Breton to as far south as Vineyard Haven. He made detailed charts of the area, over 1,000 miles of coastline. He founded Quebec, the first permanent French settlement in the new world. In a search for a northwest passage, Champlain discovered two of the Great Lakes, as well as the lake which now bears his name. He wrote many accounts of his travels and his map of 1612 was the first made of interior America.

The Pilgrims landed at Plymouth in 1620, but some twenty expeditions sailed along the New England coast before that time. Of this number, at least six sailed into Plymouth harbor. Five maps were made of the Plymouth area by 1616.

Champlain made a detailed map of the harbor in 1605. It was a quick sketch which showed evidence of many Indian houses and cornfields occupying much of the high land above the shore of the harbor.

In 1614, John Smith sailed into Plymouth Harbor. His map was the best known of New England of that period and was used, along with his writings, by the Pilgrims. He named New England, Plimouth (Plymouth), Massachusetts, the Charles River and Cape Ann, and was the first to publish these names.

John Smith also did much of the survey work from which maps of the Virginia region were drawn. Crosses marked the limit of exploration. Beyond this, the material on the map was based on Indian reports. Indian villages were marked by distinctive symbols. Most of the place names were given by Smith, as were those on his New England map.

As the French moved into the interior of America, they recorded their travels on maps. The journeys of Marquette and Joliet produced many fine maps as Joliet was an expert cartographer.

Exploration and mapping of new lands was followed by trade and settlement. East India trading companies of Holland had a "secret" atlas of 180 maps and charts and sketches

John Smith map of Virginia, 1612

for their own use. Dutch expeditions were carefully charted on maps. Each new expedition had maps of the others as a guide and each captain was required to deliver charts with his own revisions. Maps were continually improved.

Maps were not usually issued to the public until information they contained was common knowledge or until outposts had been firmly secured and adequately protected.

European map publishers of the sixteenth and seventeenth centuries were sometimes lacking in accurate information, but their maps were beautifully engraved and colored. Gold

22

and silver leaf was often applied. The *cartouche,* an ornamental design to enclose a map title, was covered with human figures, cherubs, fluted columns, fruit or other symbols. Highly detailed perspective views of villages, towns and other scenes were often included on maps.

Wind roses, which showed compass directions, were usually divided into eight primary winds. They were black on the chart. Half-winds, which subdivided them, were green and quarter-winds red. Now the usual compass rose is marked off in 360 parts or degrees.

Discovery and exploration brought a new era of adventure. From the Spanish colonies in the New World came a constant flow of precious metals. Pack trains loaded with gold and silver toiled over high mountains to the sea. Spanish galleons lay at anchor waiting to carry the treasure back to Spain. So many treasure ships traveled over the Caribbean Sea that it was called the "Spanish Main." Pirates of many nationalities lay in wait to capture and plunder. Charts were valuable so they were weighted with lead to make them easy to get rid of in case of attack.

Wind Rose

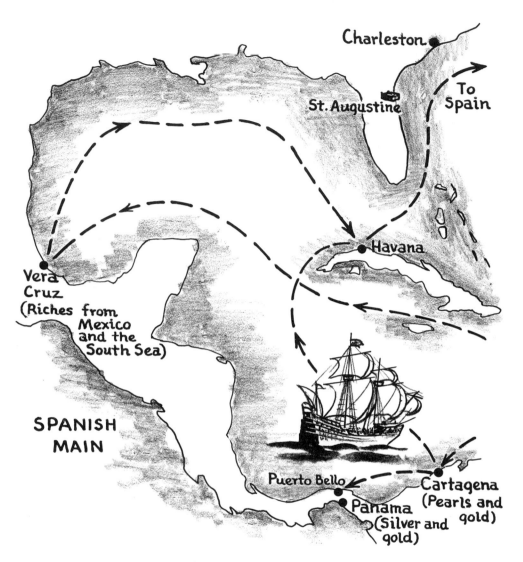

Would you like to search for buried treasure?

Millions of dollars of gold and silver still rest on the bottom of the Caribbean Sea in the sunken ships. Many locations are known and are recorded on maps. Such maps also locate the possible hiding places of treasure chests of such colorful pirates as John Laffite and Edward Teach (Blackbeard). In the "Atlas of Treasure Maps," by F. L. Coffman, over 3,000

24

locations of lost, buried or sunken treasures are marked. Today skindivers examine the wrecks of ancient galleons and bring up encrusted coins, pottery and jewelry from the sea.

In the last part of the eighteenth century Captain James Cook, an expert surveyor, was put in charge of several British expeditions to the Pacific Ocean. His three voyages charted great numbers of islands throughout the Pacific. He set new standards in the survey and charting of unknown coasts. Cook's ships crisscrossed the Pacific. He sailed from Plymouth in 1768, and charted 2,400 miles of coast around New Zealand. In 1778, Cook charted 3,000 miles along the western coast of North America from what is now Oregon to beyond the Bering Sea. His charts were drawn in a continuous survey from his ship.

By the middle of the nineteenth century the first work of exploration was complete. Lewis and Clark had brought back in 1806 enough data on the west to fill seven printed volumes. The maps they made were accurate and of great value.

They were followed by Major John Wesley Powell, the first of the field geographers in the United States. He saw a need for a survey or program of mapping which would increase knowledge and open up the new lands to settlement. Powell observed and mapped rock layers as he journeyed down the Green River to the Colorado. Grand Canyon was mapped in 1869. He classified landforms or the shape of the earth's surface — its mountains, valleys, plains and plateaus. Then he tried to determine what they meant in terms of the people who were to live in the new land. Powell wondered, and tried to determine, what part of the land could be irrigated and how rainfall drained off the land — and made maps to show these things. He was also interested in man's effect on the land.

The two great polar regions remained unexplored. In 1909, after over twenty years of arctic exploration, Robert E. Peary reached the North Pole. Richard E. Byrd, who was to make

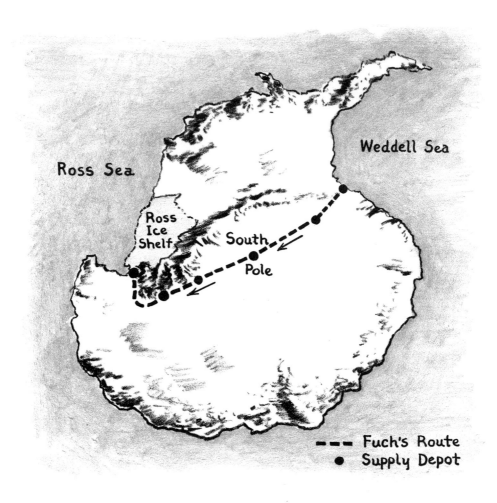

Ross Sea

Weddell Sea

Ross
Ice
Shelf

South
Pole

- - - Fuch's Route
● Supply Depot

many expeditions to the South Pole, was the first to fly over
the North Pole. With the work of these explorers, the true
character of the icecaps and polar ice pack gradually became
known and recorded on maps.

The last great continent to be explored was the Antarctic.
Cook had sailed around Antarctica, on his voyage of 1772-
1775, without ever sighting it. Then, in the middle of the
nineteenth century, several voyages were made which mapped
parts of the Antarctic coast and located and named the two

great seas, the Weddell and Ross Seas. Experienced survey-ors were in charge of these expeditions and they were well charted.

In the twentieth century the mapping of the south polar region has been carried even farther. By the time of the International Geophysical Year in 1957-58, most of the shore-line of the Antarctic had been charted. During these years eleven nations set up stations on the continent for scientific studies. Large inland areas were mapped and weather maps were made.

In 1958, a British expedition under the command of Dr. Vivian Fuchs made the first crossing of the continent, 2,250 miles across ice and snow. Scientists used explosion echoes to determine ice thickness and the level of the land beneath the ice, which they found to be as much as 13,000 feet thick in places.

3.   Where in the World

Ships that sailed the seas to all parts of the earth needed some way of locating their position, just as you or I need a road map to find our way from city to city or a street map to find the location of a particular home or business.

Hipparchus, a Greek astronomer and mathematician who lived over a hundred years before the birth of Christ, divided the earth into evenly spaced lines called latitude and longitude. These marked off the globe into 360 equal parts or *degrees*. Each degree is equal to 60 nautical miles, or approximately 69.5 land miles. Each degree is further divided into 60 *minutes*, so that one minute equals one nautical mile. Then each minute is divided into 60 *seconds*, or approximately 100 feet. By using this pattern of degrees, minutes and seconds, any point on the globe can be located precisely by its latitude and longitude. A given longitude reading will intersect a given latitude reading at only one point on the map.

What is latitude? A round ball has no beginning or end, no top or bottom, but the round earth is different. It has an imaginary line, or axis, running through its center from the North Pole to the South Pole. The earth revolves on this axis like a spinning top. Latitude is marked off first by a line circling the earth midway between the poles. We call this the *equator*. Lines of latitude are evenly spaced circles parallel to the equator. These are called *parallels,* which makes them easy to remember.

The equator is 0°. The poles are 90°. A position north of the equator is North Latitude; a point south of the equator is South Latitude. You will notice on the drawing of latitude that the distance around each parallel gets shorter as one moves from the equator to the poles. Sixty degrees latitude is one-half the length of the equator.

Lines of longitude are evenly spaced lines radiating out from the poles and meeting at the equator. These are called *meridians*. They are of equal length. Many starting points have been used in numbering these merdians. Most countries now

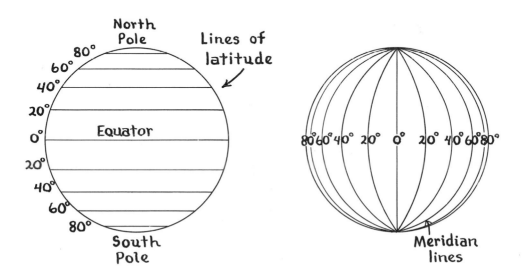

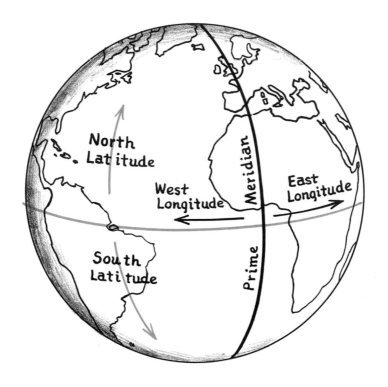

use Greenwich, England, as 0° or the Prime Meridian. Everything east of this line is East Longitude; everything west of it is West Longitude. Each side is numbered from 0° to 180°. The 180° meridian is on the opposite side of the earth from the Prime Meridian and is called the International Date Line.

Meridians are often numbered by 15° on maps that divide the world into time zones. Why? Because the earth takes 24 hours to make a complete 360° turn. As the earth rotates, the position of the sun changes above it. Every four minutes it will move 1°; each hour it turns 15°, and the noonday sun will have moved directly overhead another 15° of longitude. You can see that longitude and time are closely related. When it is noon on the Prime Meridian, it is midnight on the International Date Line. Another new day is about to begin.

Instruments were needed to determine the exact lines of

30

latitude and longitude. The early *astrolabe* was a circular disc marked off into 360 degrees. The sun was sighted along a moveable arm attached to its center. A more refined version of the astrolabe is the *sextant*. It is sighted on the horizon and the North Star. The angle formed gives the latitude in degrees.

It was many years before longitude could be accurately determined. Since 15° equals one hour of time, all that was really needed was a very accurate timepiece. But clocks at the time of Columbus were bulky and not very accurate.

The *chronometer* solved the problem. It was invented by John Harrison in England about the middle of the eighteenth century. This clock was so accurate that after weeks at sea it would not be off more than a few seconds daily. It was first used by James Cook about the time of the American Revolution. Since then it has been possible to determine both latitude and longitude with the same degree of accuracy.

Before a ship starts out on a voyage, the chronometer is set at exactly noon, sun time, which is when the sun does not cast a shadow either to the east or the west. As the ship travels east or west of this point, the difference in time between noon at the first point and noon at the new location is noted. Each hour of difference in time between places represents 15° of longitude. Time signals are now flashed by radio from Greenwich, so that even greater accuracy is possible.

Now, with our series of parallels and meridians and accurate methods of computing our position in relation to these imaginary lines, we can be as sure of our position in the middle of the Pacific as you are at the main corner in your town. But although we have learned how we find position on a map, for a map to be really useful we will need to know *direction*. North is, by custom, usually at the top of a map, but it may be in any other direction or even in the center.

If you happen to be a Boy Scout or Girl Scout, you have probably used a compass and may already know that there is a difference between the true north of the North Pole and the magnetic north toward which the compass needle points. This difference is known as *compass declination* and is indicated on most large-scale maps intended to be used outdoors. A drawing of a single spear with a barb on the end usually indicates magnetic north; some maps will show both true north and magnetic north.

The magnetic poles are 1,400 miles away from the geographic poles. The compass needle varies in its deviation from true north, depending on where one is located. In order to know true north, we must know how much the compass needle turns away from it, or its declination in our particular locality. Using the arrow — the spear with a barb — you can place your compass on the map and determine the exact position of both the north directions. Another way is to line up landmarks on your map with the real landmarks on the earth around you and thus check your compass declination.

If you happen to live near Cincinnati, Ohio, or anywhere else on the line of zero magnetic declination, your compass will point to true north. This is the *agonic line*, where true north and the north of the compass needle coincide. It is marked 0° on the declination map, but has no relationship to 0° longitude. East of the agonic line, the compass north points in a westerly direction; west of the line it points in an easterly direction. Since the earth's magnetism is constantly changing, maps have to be redrawn frequently in order to be completely accurate and up-to-date in showing compass declination.

The shortest distance between two points on the globe is not a straight line, but a *great circle*. This is the name given any circle which cuts the globe in two equal parts as does the equator. All meridians cut the globe in half, and are therefore great circles. The equator is the only parallel that is a great circle.

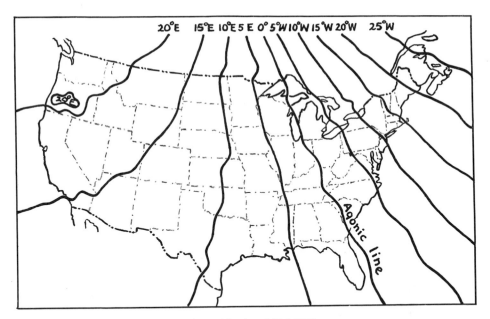

DECLINATION CHART

Philadelphia, Pennsylvania, and Ankara, Turkey, are on the same parallel of latitude, yet this line of latitude would not represent the shortest distance between the two cities. A great circle, even though it goes north of this line, would be the shortest distance.

One of the most important features of any map is its *scale*. A map is a simplified picture of the earth very much reduced in size. To understand a map and relate it to actual size of the area mapped, we need to know just how much it has been reduced in size — or, in other words, what its scale is.

Scale is expressed in several ways on maps. *Numerical scale* is probably the most common. It is written as a ratio, using the colon mark to mean "to." If a map's scale is 1 to 10,000, it is written 1:10,000 which means that one unit of measure on the map is equal to 10,000 of the same unit on the ground or other area mapped. This would be true whether the unit of measure be inches, meters or even jelly beans.

33

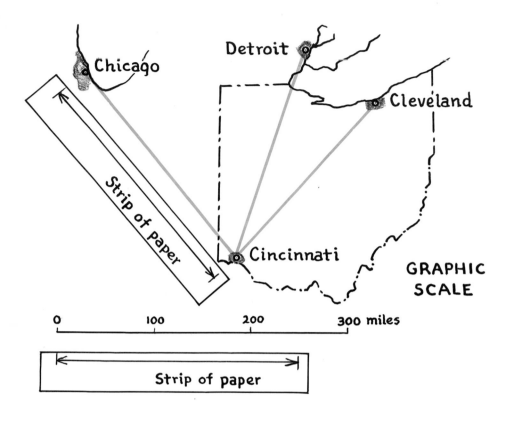

Chicago

Detroit

Cleveland

Strip of paper

Cincinnati

GRAPHIC
SCALE

0   100   200   300 miles

Strip of paper

Suppose you have a map of Alaska which is 1:5,000,000. If it were possible to enlarge this map 5,000,000 times, your map could fit right over the state of Alaska!

There are 63,360 inches in a mile. So 1:63,360 is the same as one inch equals one mile, which is the way a scale is often made.

Perhaps you are interested in making scale models of ships or airplanes. If you have built a ship model which is 500 feet to an inch, the proportion would be 1 to 6,000 (12 inches equals one foot; 500 x 12 = 6,000). So if your map were on the same scale of 1:6,000, your little model ship could be placed on the water area and would be in exact proportion to the map as the actual ship would be to the world. It might

34

be interesting to combine your models with a large-scale map made on the same scale. Ships could steam into harbors and planes land at airports.

Another kind of scale is the *graphic scale*. It shows the scale on a line which represents a certain number of miles on the earth. It is usually shown in round numbers. If a map with this scale is reduced or enlarged by photograph or photostat, the scale remains true. You can easily check the distance between two points on a map with a graphic scale. Take a piece of paper with a straight edge and place it on the map as shown in the illustration. Mark the positions of A and B. Now by placing the paper along the graphic scale, you can easily determine the distance between the two points.

One word of caution. When maps are drawn in small scale, many measurements are not completely accurate. Maps with a scale of 1 to 1,000,000 or smaller are the types usually found in an atlas. The *larger* the number, the *smaller* the scale. The *smaller* the number, the *larger* the scale and the greater amount of detail will be shown on the map.

Should there be no scale on a map, you can figure one out by measuring the latitude. One degree of latitude equals approximately 69 miles. Thus, if you measure 10 degrees latitude, that measurement would equal 690 miles on the map. Be sure to take your measurement from near the center of the map as it will be most accurate there.

4.   Mapping the Seas that Surround Us

More than two-thirds of the surface of our earth is covered by the oceans, yet until recent years this has remained largely an unknown world.

During the International Geophysical Year — IGY — which lasted through half of 1957 and all of 1958, seventy-five ships of twenty-six nations explored the oceans. Scientists probed the depths of the seas at many levels. Sounding instruments, wave recorders, tide gauges and other instruments were busy recording masses of information about underwater areas. The resulting figures are helping to map the patterns of the ocean depths.

One item of special interest about the sea is its movement. Perhaps the best-known current is the Gulf Stream which flows out of the Caribbean along the east coast of Florida and southern United States, then veers northeast across the Atlantic

Ocean. This current is 50 miles wide and 1,500 feet deep. It carries along about 1,000 times as much water as the Mississippi River at a speed of about five or ten miles a day.

Benjamin Franklin made the first dependable map of the Gulf Stream. First he obtained data about Atlantic currents from whalers. Then he added observations of his own, made during several ocean crossings. Ships had crossed the Atlantic for nearly 300 years and a pattern of currents was beginning to emerge.

Today our maps show surface currents throughout the world. Deep currents are less familiar. The Gulf Stream flows *north*, yet it was not until 1957 that a huge deep current a mile-and-a-half below the Gulf Stream was found flowing *south* from the Arctic. Since then oceanographers have discovered other deep currents and marked their positions on maps.

Along our shores the Geodetic Survey attaches instruments to buoys to record the direction and speed of ocean currents. Other tests made of ocean waters are for temperature and the salinity, or amount of salt in the water. Maps show speed and direction of both tidal and ocean currents. Monthly temperature charts are issued, and other maps show polar ice conditions. *Bottom sediment* charts show the character of the sea

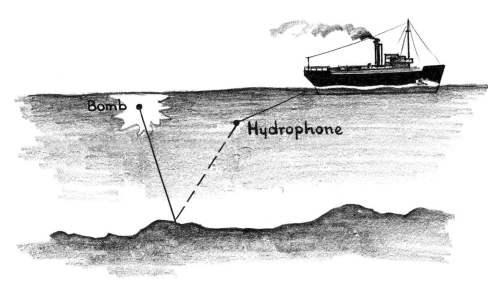

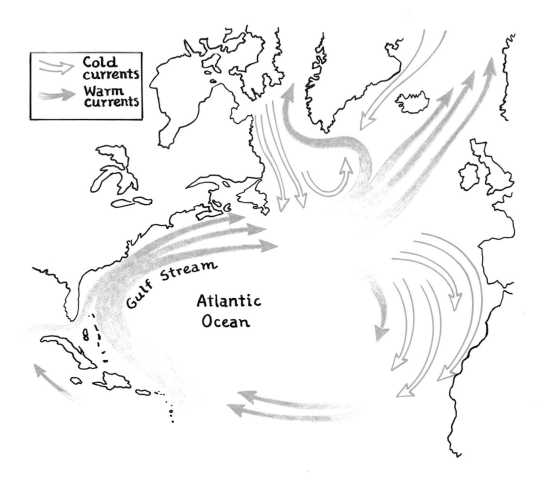

Gulf Stream

Atlantic
Ocean

bottom in water less than 100 fathoms (600 feet) deep. Such data is usually overprinted on standard navigational charts.

The most important tool for measuring the oceans is the *fathometer*. It charts the shape of the ocean bottom. An operator aboard a vessel listens on headphones as three pounds of TNT is exploded just beneath the surface of the water. Depth is charted by measuring the time it takes the signal to travel to the bottom and return. A continuous series of impulses is recorded on moving graph paper, making a map of the ocean floor as the ship moves over it.

Sediment over 500 feet deep may be measured by its double echo. The difference in time between the echo which bounces off the top of the sediment and the echo that bounces off the bottom gives its thickness.

Position readings or bearings must be accurately taken so that the recorded depths may be correctly plotted on the chart.

The ocean bottom itself is sometimes penetrated by 10-foot weighted coring tubes which bring up samples of the bottom. Dredges scoop up rocks and deep-sea cameras photograph the sea bottom, revealing marine life found there.

In early 1960, the *Trieste*, a strange clumsy looking object called a *bathyscaph*, dropped down into the ocean depths off the Mariana Islands in the Pacific Ocean. Inside a small gondola were two men, one Lieutenant Don Walsh of the United States Navy, the other Jacques Piccard, son of the man who had developed the bathyscaph. Rough soundings had shown the bottom to be 33,600 feet, but it was not until approximately 37,800 feet that the bathyscaph softly hit the ocean floor, raising a cloud of silt. After observing life on the bottom, the men dropped ballast and returned to the surface.

The ocean depths are of increasing importance, especially to submarines. As these underwater craft probe deeper and

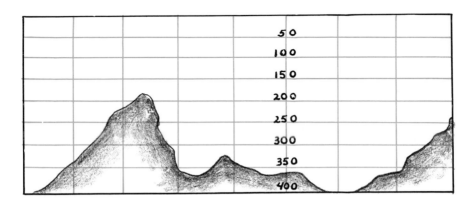

Echo sounding contour as recorded on graph paper

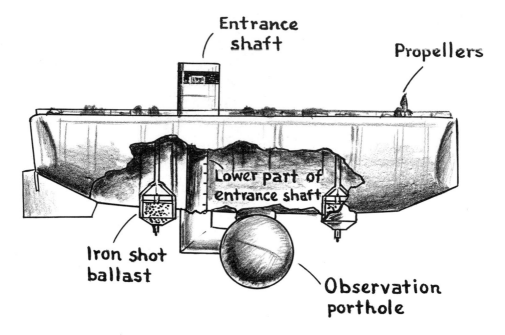

Entrance shaft

Propellers

Lower part of entrance shaft

Iron shot ballast

Observation porthole

Diagram of bathyscaph

deeper, new information is needed on water temperature, currents and the ocean bottom. The *Trieste* proved that the ocean bottom could now be reached, explored, and accurately mapped, even at its deepest points.

If there were a drain in the deepest part of the ocean and we were to pull out the plug, the ocean bottom would stand revealed like the land. We would see a landscape in form much like the one we are familiar with. We would see great peaks, (even higher than any on land), canyons to rival Grand Canyon, cliffs, plateaus and plains. Mapping this underwater world will be a challenge for years to come. We have just begun to make detailed maps of the ocean floor showing its form. Many surprising features will undoubtedly be discovered. In recent years, large sinkholes one-half mile across and 500 feet deep were found off the tip of Florida in 1,000 feet of water.

Along the Atlantic coast of the United States, the *Continental shelf* extends 150 to 175 miles, then plunges 8,000 feet in a huge submarine cliff. Here begins the deep sea bottom. Submarine canyons cut the shelf at several places.

The *mid-Atlantic ridge* runs the length of the North and South Atlantic, stretching well over one-third of the way around the earth. It lies submerged a mile below the water's surface, yet it rises two miles from the ocean bottom. Other mountain chains run through the oceans, one of the last to be discovered being a range extending from northern Greenland past the North Pole to Russia.

Such submarine features represent permanent landmarks. When the contours, or outlines, of these underwater mountains are accurately placed on charts, the navigator may find his position by using a fathometer. He records a number of depth soundings and distances. These are then plotted on a strip of transparent paper on the same scale as the chart, producing outlines of the ridges and valleys below the surface. The paper can be matched to the corresponding areas on the chart to locate the position of the vessel. In time of bad weather or poor radio reception, depth-curve navigators can give a fairly accurate position.

In 1957, the Coast and Geodetic Survey celebrated its 150th anniversary. It does much of the work of mapping and charting the water of the United States and its possessions. Recently its surveys have been extended to the continental shelf and beyond.

The Hydrographic Office, a part of the Navy department, maps and publishes about 6,000 charts covering the navigable waters of the world.

Many aids are necessary to make the waters safe for navigation. These are marked on *nautical charts*. On these charts, lighthouse symbols dot our shores. Lighthouses are usually placed less than forty miles apart so that their lights may be

Atlantic Ocean depths

visible by ships approaching the shore at any point. Twenty-four lightships — floating lighthouses — are stationed off our coasts. Ambrose lightship lies at 40° 49′ W. longitude, or about twenty miles southwest of Manhattan. Nantucket lightship rides at anchor off Nantucket Island. These two lightships, along with others, help guide transatlantic vessels into New York harbor. But the days of the lightship are almost over. All but two are being replaced by Texas Towers, skeleton-beamed steel platforms, set solidly into the ocean bottom. Some towers will have a five-man crew, and a roof for helicopter landings; others will be unmanned, remote-controlled from shore.

There are over 3,400 lighted buoys being maintained in United States waters. Navigators check the position of their ships by checking the position of these buoys as shown on their navigation charts.

Radio beacons send out signals from most lighthouses and lightships. A ship's position may be found by plotting three radio beacon bearings on a chart.

Apparatus for receiving these signals is carried on all modern passenger ships and many other vessels. There are four

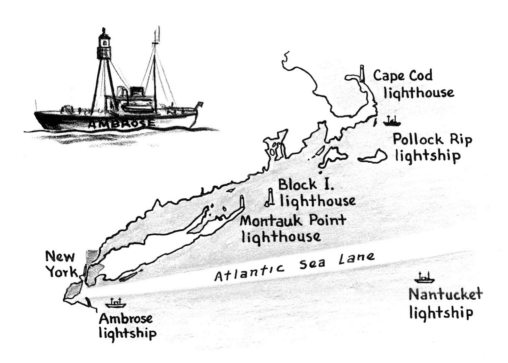

Position of major lightships and lighthouses along southern New England coast

43

classes of beacons ranging from Class A, which has a reliable range of 200 miles, to Class D with a reliable range of about 10 miles.

LORAN, a newer development, is for long range navigation, and derives its name from the first letters of those words. With this system, ships may find their position in minutes when within 750 nautical miles of the transmitting stations. The receiving set on board ship measures the time differences between radio signals from sending stations on shore. The navigator finds the exact curve printed on the LORAN chart for each. His ship's position is the point at which they cross.

Transit IB, the first successful navigation satellite, offers the promise of accurate direction and distance finding, especially for submarine missile firing. The Navy plans four satellites to cover the earth completely.

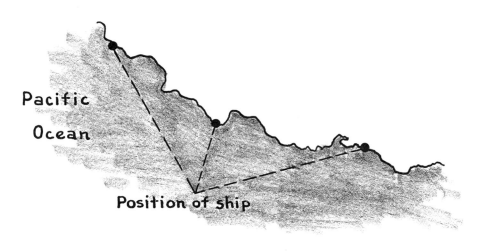

Radio beams plotted on chart

5.   Mapping the Land Beneath Our Feet

George Washington realized the need for more accurate maps while General of the Army. He obtained help from the Continental Congress which authorized him to appoint someone to survey and sketch the country.

Washington himself was an experienced surveyor and mapmaker. When only fourteen years of age, he drew an accurate picture of a chain, compass and scale. He surveyed over 200 tracts in his lifetime. Traveling far and wide over the eastern United States, he made eight journeys through New England and over 250 in Maryland and Virginia. Washington used a standard surveyor's chain of 66 feet. A steel tape of 100 or 200 feet has since replaced the chain.

Measuring the distance between two points is not as simple as you might think. As long as the tape is used on clear, level land, it is easy to get accurate measurements. But suppose we want to measure hilly or mountainous land. Then we have a problem. Our tape would go up and down, but what we want is level ground measurement.

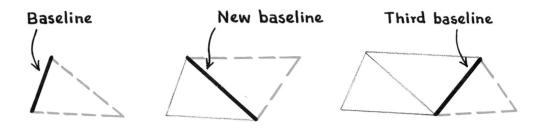

Baseline   New baseline   Third baseline

Measuring the land by triangulation

We also need to consider the curve of the earth's surface. If you were to lie flat beside a bay which is ten miles across, with your eyes at the level of the water, a five-story building on the opposite shore would be just below your eye level — because of the curvature of the earth.

The study of the mathematics of the size and shape of the earth is called *geodesy*. If the earth were a perfect sphere, the problem of curvature would be relatively simple. But the earth is flattened at the poles and, according to the latest findings, slightly pear-shaped. This calls for very precise measurements over long distances.

To overcome difficulties of terrain and to speed up surveying of mountainous or hilly regions, a method called *triangulation* is used. It had been known for many years that if you know the length of one side of a triangle and the size of two of the angles, you could figure the length of the other two sides without measuring them. Triangulation makes use of this fact.

The first step in triangulation is measuring that first side of a triangle, the base line. This must be a fairly level area — often a straight road or railroad is used. A stake is driven into the ground at each end of the surveyor's tape. To keep

46

the tape from sagging, it is stretched tight with a spring scale until it has a pull of thirty-three pounds. Moving the tape along, the entire distance of the base line is measured, then checked by measuring backward, and double-checked. Often surveyors work with no more than 1/16 inch error to a mile.

Once the base line is exact, angles from it are determined by means of a *theodolite,* a telescope with an angle-measuring device. Precise measurements are important. The survey party selects routes of triangulation so that angle observations can be made from high points of land or hilltops; trees or other obstructions are cleared.

A portable *Bilby tower* made of steel or aluminum may be used when a suitable high observation point is not available. Easily set up and dismantled, the tower can be erected as high as 130 feet. It is really two towers, one within the other. The inner tower supports a theodolite; the outer tower supports two platforms, the lower one for the observer and his

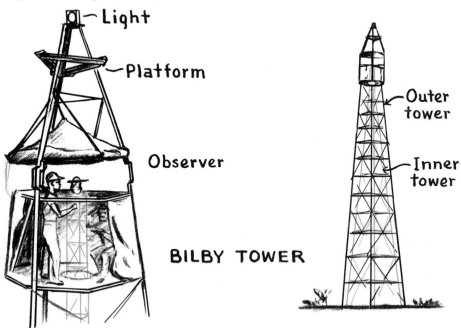

Light

Platform

Observer

BILBY TOWER

Outer tower

Inner tower

recorder, the upper for the lightkeeper who controls the signal lamp at the peak of the tower. As the triangulation party goes forward, new towers are set up ahead, rear ones dismantled.

With a base line and two angles known, the measurements of a complete triangle are known, and one of the new sides can be used as a new base line for another triangle. Level ground measurement is obtained without actually measuring it foot by foot, and the information is recorded on maps. Surveying parties could go on across the country this way were it not for the fact that errors increase. After several dozen triangles have been determined, a control base line is measured off again to check the accuracy.

This triangulation network which crisscrosses the land is called *first order triangulation*. The sides of the triangles measured are 15 to 40 miles long. But the points determined are too far apart for detailed mapping, so *second order triangulation* establishes points within the original network. Observations for first and second order triangulation are usually taken at night when there is less atmospheric disturbance. Heat waves make long-range observation inaccurate.

Signaling can be done by theodolite. A brightly colored cloth cone over the instrument helps to identify its position. The sun can also be used for signaling by the use of a *heliotrope*. Series of mirrors catch the sunlight and aim it at a distant point where the flash is plotted. If the sun is not strong enough, powerful electric lights may be used.

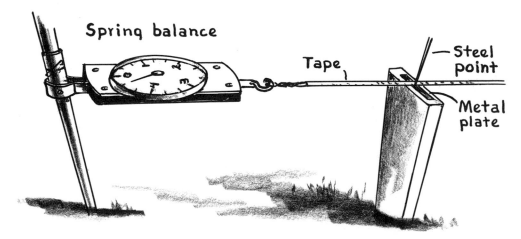

Spring balance

Tape

Steel point

Metal plate

Distance is determined in several ways. A *tellurometer* measures by a comparison of modulated radio waves between two units. A *geodimeter* is used at night. It measures the time it takes a beam of light to travel to a group of mirrors and back again. This time is then converted to miles.

The Army Map Service is attempting to map most of the world. Base lines are run through dense jungles, from one mountaintop to another or across ice fields. Cargo planes and helicopters take map-makers and their gear to remote areas. Portable radio or sometimes light signals at night are used to keep units in contact with one another.

Leveling determines the exact altitude or distance above sea level of an area, and this information is recorded on maps also. Leveling parties employ the principles of triangulation, although they work independently of triangulation parties, since they are concerned with lower levels. They follow roads, railways and rivers, and their progress is slower.

You have probably seen a carpenter's level. By tipping it up or down slightly, the little bubble moves away from the center line. A leveling instrument works in the same way, but in this case the level bubble is attached to a telescope and readings are made from a graduated measuring rod. Measurements are made at a distance of not more than 500 feet, although if the land is steep or uneven, they may need to be much closer. As the leveling progresses, readings are taken forward and backward to check the accuracy.

The pattern of triangulation is called *horizontal control*. Leveling is called *vertical control*. A program to survey the entire country with first and second order triangulation and first and second order levels is nearly complete. A large map of the United States shows the status of horizontal control, another the status of vertical control.

Station marks giving data of triangulation and *bench marks* giving leveling information are placed in permanent locations

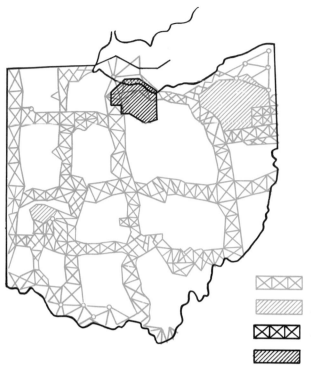

STATUS OF
HORIZONTAL
CONTROL (OHIO)

⊠⊠⊠	Adjusted first-order triangulation
⫽⫽⫽	Adjusted second-order triangulation
⊠⊠⊠	Unadjusted first-order triangulation
⫽⫽⫽	Unadjusted second-order triangulation

for future reference. Where no permanent feature exists at the proper location — such as a large rock or permanent masonry structure — a concrete monument is made by pouring concrete into a hole dug below frost line. A bronze tablet or disc is set flush with the top of the monument and another four feet below ground level.

Local surveyors use these marks as a base for local surveys. Locating one of these marks is a bit like following a map to buried treasure. A description of one of these located in Hasbrouck Heights, New Jersey, follows:

"On an island in the center of Rte. 6 at its intersection with Collins Ave.; 68.76 ft. easterly from a cup tack, about 1 ft. up on the west side of pole #60735-HBH, situated on the southerly side of Rte. 6; 54.60 ft. easterly from a cross cut on the rim of a manhole located just west of a triangle at entrance to Collins Ave., on the southerly side of Rte. 6; 35.23 ft. southerly from a cross cut on the rim of a manhole located in westerly

STATUS OF
VERTICAL
CONTROL
(OHIO)

_____ First-order leveling
- - - - Second-order leveling
• Additional second-order
leveling within this area

travelled lane of Rtc. 6; 19.12 ft. westerly from a cross cut on slab #789-B also located in westerly travelled lane of said Rte. 6, flush with the ground. A standard N. J. 6. C. S. disc, set in concrete. Elevation 92.763 feet."

The network of triangulation is filled in with third and fourth-order triangulation, often done by the United States Geological Survey or by state surveys.

Airplane photography has moved the mapping of the world ahead many years. With it we can map formerly inaccessible lands such as the tropical forests of the Amazon River and the frozen wastes of the Antarctic. In a week's time an area the size of Pennsylvania can be photographed and completely mapped.

Aerial photos are used in many ways. The geologist can tell something of what lies beneath the surface. The archaeologist uses aerial photographs to detect buried cities and buildings which often show up clearly where buried masonry reduces

51

the crop above it. City maps, which would take at least months or possibly years by ordinary methods, are made in a few hours.

Battles have been lost or won, depending upon the accuracy of air reconnaissance. Planes flying at high speeds close to the ground can take continuous photographs which are synchronized to the plane's speed. They reproduce sharp and clear pictures. Other planes flying so high they are invisible to the naked eye take pictures of remarkable clarity. U-2 planes flying over Russia at 80,000 feet have photographed large areas in a few hours. Such photographs show pinpoint detail so that extremely accurate maps may be made from them.

The government publishes a large map showing the status of aerial photography throughout the entire country. The various government agencies or private companies concerned with a particular region are listed, and you can obtain aerial photos of your own town by writing to the agency that covers your area.

Airplane photographs usually cover only a few square miles.

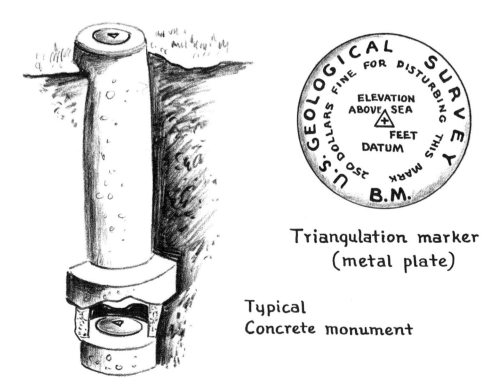

U.S. GEOLOGICAL SURVEY
$250 DOLLARS FINE FOR DISTURBING THIS MARK
ELEVATION
ABOVE SEA
FEET
DATUM
B.M.

Triangulation marker
(metal plate)

Typical
Concrete monument

If we match together two or more overlapping aerial photos, we have "mosaics" available which are indicated on a government map showing the status of aerial mosaics. Such map coverage of the United States is spotty.

New instruments and methods are constantly being developed for mapping the earth with more accuracy and speed. One day the entire earth will be mapped accurately and in great detail.

6. How Do You Like Your Mountains?

The problems of showing accurate and realistic *relief* —
mountains, hills and valleys — is one which has always troubled
the map-maker. If you have ever taken an automobile trip
across the Rocky Mountains and then flown across these same
mountains by jet plane you would notice how much they
"flatten out" when seen from above. Grand Canyon, a mile-
deep gash in the earth, seems almost flat when viewed from
high above.

When a map-maker further reduces the area to the size of
a small map, he runs into trouble. Mountains and hills done

54

in exact scale are often too small even to be recognized. If exaggerated, mountains either have to be spread over a larger area, combined and simplified, or brought up into needle-sharp peaks which distort true shape.

One of the best solutions to this problem of showing the irregular surface of the land is the *topographic* map which uses *contour lines* to show relief. Contour lines are imaginary lines, every point of which is at the same altitude above sea level. You have probably played the game where you draw lines from one numbered dot to another without knowing what your finished picture will be. Perhaps you end up with a clown, a cowboy or a dog. The cartographer does something very similar when he draws contour lines.

The water line of a lake or other large body of water is a contour line in itself, since water finds its own level and the surface of the body of water is all at the same altitude above sea level. You have no doubt seen the line left around a pond

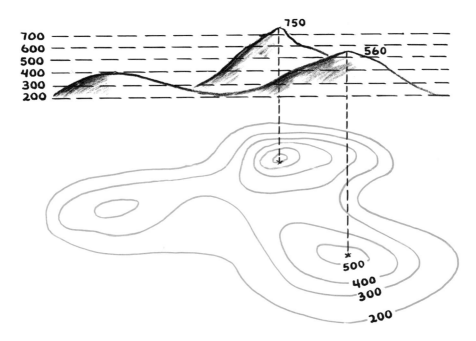

when the water level drops. Even the ring around your bath-tub is a contour line.

Contours are drawn at regular intervals of elevation. On large-scale and medium-scale maps in flat country they may be only five feet apart; in mountains, as much as 100 feet apart. Usually every fifth contour is made heavier and shows the altitude above sea level. It may help you to visualize contours if you realize that water flowing downhill will flow *across* the imaginary contour lines. But the best way to learn to read a topographic map is to take one in hand and compare it with the actual landscape. After doing this with several maps, you should be able to "see" the landscape simply by looking at a contour map.

Over 21,000 topographic maps have been published for the United States and are available to the public. Yet less than half of the United States is mapped adequately for modern needs of engineering projects, industrial development and road constructiton.

A *Status of Topographic Maps,* which can be obtained free from the Geological Survey, will show you what maps are available throughout the country. A more detailed index can be obtained of your own state. Should you want to purchase a map of your own town or local area, the cost is very low. Your own house may be included on the map.

The National Topographic Map Series has a new series of small-scale maps, 1:250,000, which cover most of the country. Each year a number of older maps are revised and brought up to date. Large-scale maps cover many densely populated regions and other areas needing detailed information for en-gineering, industry, irrigation and other large projects.

Topographic symbols usually appear in the following colors: black for cultural, or man-made, features such as buildings and power lines; blue for water features; brown for relief, contour lines, sandy areas; green for vegetation; and red for roads. Scales

56

TOPOGRAPHIC MAP SYMBOLS

SYMBOLS

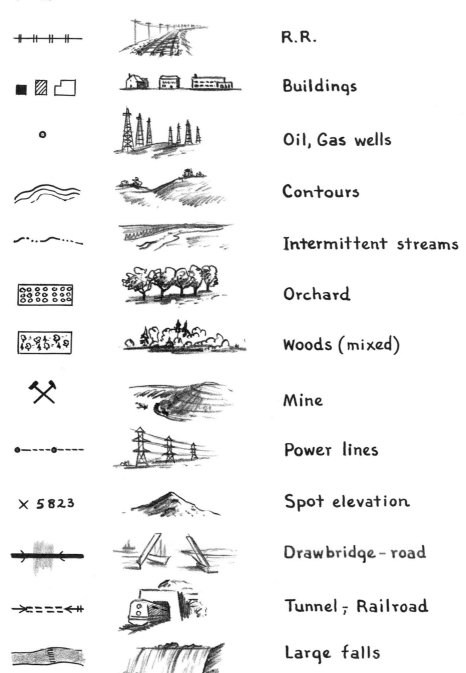

R.R.

Buildings

Oil, Gas wells

Contours

Intermittent streams

Orchard

Woods (mixed)

Mine

Power lines

X 5823   Spot elevation

Drawbridge - road

Tunnel; Railroad

Large falls

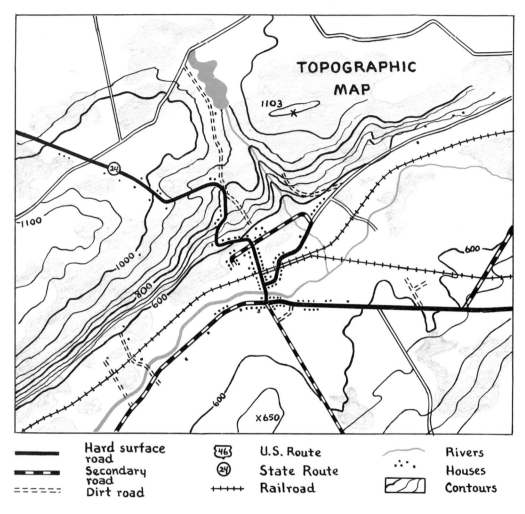

TOPOGRAPHIC MAP

1103

1100

1000

800

600

600

600

X650

▬▬▬	Hard surface road	46	U.S. Route	⌒⌒	Rivers	
▬▫▬	Secondary road	24	State Route	∴	Houses	
≡≡≡≡	Dirt road	+++++	Railroad	▱	Contours	

vary in the National Topographic Series from 1:1,000,000 to 1:24,000. Topographic sheets are usually named after the map's outstanding cultural feature, often its most prominent city or town. The geographic location name indicates the county, state or general geographic area of the map.

The use of contour lines is one of several methods for showing *landforms*, or relief. Other kinds of maps show mountains and other elevations by *hatchures*. In this system, the hills or mountains are shaded with closely set lines. Water would *fol-*

58

low the direction of these lines as it runs down a slope. When the slope is steeper, lines are thicker or closer together.

Altitude tints are used on small-scale maps and give a very generalized picture, not of specific landforms but of altitudes above sea level. The contour lines are drawn and the spaces between them are painted in different colored tints or tones of gray.

A *shaded relief map* is rendered in tones of gray or other color so that the relief looks like a photograph. It is the most realistic of all methods. One of the best methods for showing relief is a combination of contour lines and shaded relief. Government maps of the states and national parks feature this kind of map.

Landform maps show by means of pictorial relief symbols of the landscape as seen from above. Landform symbols indicate different kinds of mountains, glacial deposits, plateaus and other landforms. Sometimes symbols indicating vegetation are added to the map.

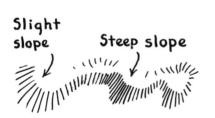

Hatchures

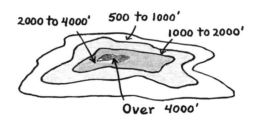

Altitude tints

Shaded relief

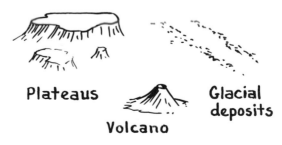

Plateaus

Volcano

Glacial deposits

Landform

The science of geology uses maps to a very great extent. You may have guessed this already, since the Geological Survey is the source of most of our topographic maps. Geology also makes use of a special kind of map known as a *block diagram*. These three-dimensional sections are drawn as though cut out of the landscape and are used to represent the landforms and underlying structure of small regions. Often they do not show an actual section of the landscape, but rather illustrate the principles of *geomorphology*, which is the science of landforms. For example, a block diagram might be used to show the development of a typical area of caverns and sinkholes. An index map of the United States shows the status of geologic mapping in this country, about one-half of which is covered.

Would you like to be able to see your country from shore to shore? You can, at Babson Institute in Wellesley Hills, Massachusetts. More than 1,200 plaster blocks, each representing a degree of latitude and longitude, have been put together to form a huge map of the United States 65 feet across. The map conforms to the curvature of the earth. It is on a scale of four miles to the inch. The relief, or vertical scale, is exaggerated six times in mountain areas, but twelve times in lowlands to bring out landforms which would otherwise be lost.

Three-dimensional relief models were used with much success during World War II. Early maps were made of plaster or of sponge rubber which could be rolled up for carrying. But even sponge rubber was expensive and clumsy to carry. How could these maps be made cheaply, quickly, light in weight and in large quantities? The answer was plastic.

The model is cut with a *pantograph router*. The operator traces a flat map, beginning with the highest elevations. As it is traced, the revolving tool moves in the same pattern over the block of plastic and cuts a layer of the plastic away. Before carving, the model is covered with a colored ocher dye

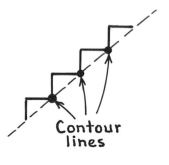

Contour lines

Tool cutting elevation

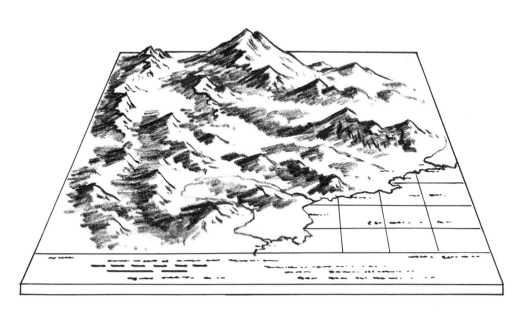

Preparing a plastic map

which remains to show the contour lines on the finished model.

The color map is printed on plastic sheets. Then these sheets are placed over a plaster landform mold of the same area. Heat and vacuum mold the plastic sheet to the mountains and valleys of the model. Once the model is made, these maps can be mass-produced. Large numbers can be shipped in a single package as they nest together.

These maps are now available for most of the northeastern part of our country. They may be purchased from the Army Map Service. Private companies also make similar maps of individual states or other areas.

Contour lines may be drawn from pairs of pictures. You have probably used a viewer which brings two images together to produce a three-dimensional picture. That is what the map-maker does. Overlapping photographs taken high in the air from slightly different positions are put in a stereoscope. Mountains stand out as if they were real. This large complex machine is called a multiple projector. The operator draws in contour lines upon the stereoscopic pairs of pictures.

7. Mapping the Air We Breathe

You have probably heard the expression "as changeable as the weather." One could also say "as changeable as the weather map." Like fingerprints, no two weather maps are exactly alike.

We have already seen that topographic maps are built up in a series of contour lines. Weather maps are made in much the same way, but with two important differences: weather maps show contours of invisible air masses, and these air masses are constantly in motion. Since the weather is always changing, weather maps are constantly in need of change.

Contour lines on a weather map surround high and low pressure areas. These lines — called *isobars* — indicate places of equal air pressure, rather than of equal altitude. Air pressures, given in millibars from each reporting station, are marked on the map. Then lines are drawn through each station having the same air pressure. When finished, the weatherman has a contour picture of "mountains" and "valleys" of air.

One thousand millibars equal 29.5 inches mercury, which is approximately normal atmospheric pressure. This is the barometric reading that you hear on your daily weather report on radio or television. When isobars are close together, the "hill" of air is steeper. Air flows faster; winds are high.

Air masses are vast bodies of air which are about the same temperature and moisture when measured across at a fixed level. These masses take on the temperature and moisture characteristics of the land over which they form.

Cold air masses form over the polar regions. Warm air masses form in the tropics. If a cold air mass pushes a warm air mass, we have a *cold front*. Its symbol has pointed teeth. If a warm air mass pushes over a cold mass, we have a *warm front*. Its symbol has rounded teeth. If the boundary between fronts does not move, we have a *stationary front*. This symbol has teeth on both sides of the line. An *occluded front* occurs when a cold front overtakes a warm front and lifts it off the ground. On the map it is shown with alternate rounded and pointed teeth. The gray tinted parts of the map show areas of rain or snow.

If we could dye these air masses — perhaps the cold ones blue and the warm ones pink — and could photograph them with a movie camera from a satellite out in space, we could see weather as it really is.

From our platform in space we would see that our weather moves across the United States from west to east. It travels about 600 miles a day — faster in winter than in summer.

We might see a mountain of cold air forming in the cold regions over Canada. A warm air mass moves in from the Caribbean Sea, heavy-laden with moisture. When these huge air masses collide, fronts are formed. Much of our bad weather occurs along such fronts.

As a cold front forms, lumpy cumulus clouds appear and quickly build up into towering thunderheads. Lightning flashes

64

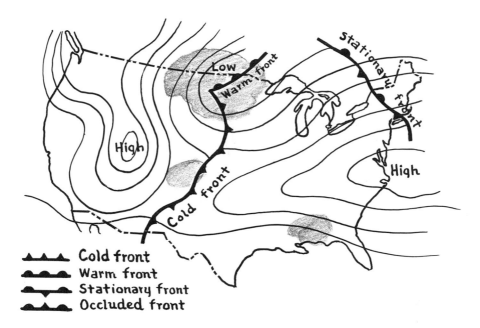

▲▲▲ Cold front
●●● Warm front
●▲● Stationary front
●▲● Occluded front

stab the air. Quick, hard showers take place. When a warm air mass overtakes a cold one, we see a warm front developing. Clouds form hundreds of miles ahead of the front as the warm pushes over the cold in a long, thin wedge. As the front moves forward, low stratus clouds bring a dull rain which may last for days.

The movement of these great air masses makes a pattern of circulation. As we look down from our imaginary satellite, we can see whirling areas of high and low pressure. High pressure areas are "mountains" of air whirling in clockwise direction. Air flowing down into low pressure "valleys" circulates in the opposite direction, or counterclockwise. These lows usually bring stormy weather.

Official U. S. Weather Bureau maps have symbols for about 200 weather stations. A closeup of one of these stations itself is marked on the map as a circle. The amount of black within the circle indicates cloudiness.

Feathered arrows "fly with the wind." They point into the circle in the direction the wind is blowing. Clustered around each station are such data as temperature, cloud type, and precipitation. Nearly 170 weather symbols show in this type of "shorthand" the state of the weather from "dust storm in sight" to "heavy thunderstorm with hail."

Some of these weather stations are lonely, isolated spots. The one on top of Mount Washington, New Hampshire, is buffeted by winds as high as 231 miles per hour. In winter it is covered with ice and snow.

How does a meteorologist go about measuring the weather that is recorded on weather maps? His most important instrument is the *barometer*, which records air pressure by the rise or fall of mercury. Temperature of air is measured by a thermometer. A special type, called a *thermograph*, keeps a continuous record on a revolving drum. A *hydrograph* measures humidity with a human hair. Dry air causes it to shrink; humid air causes it to stretch. A pen traces the changes on a moving piece of paper.

Cold front

Warm front

DAILY WEATHER MAP

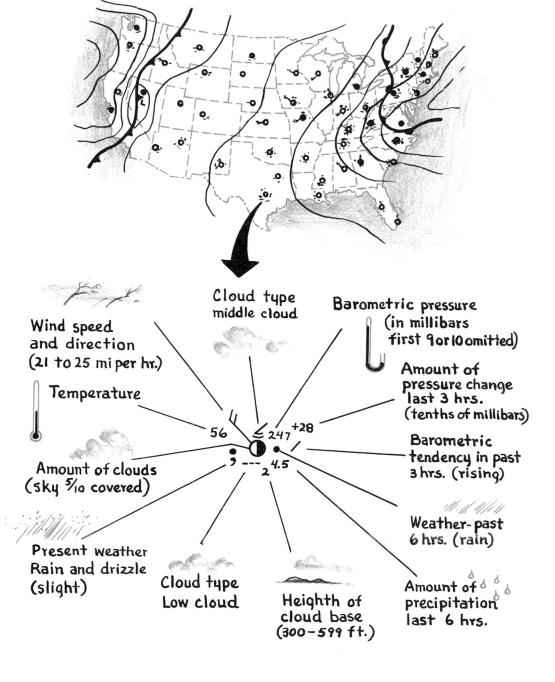

Cloud type
middle cloud

Barometric pressure
(in millibars
first 9 or 10 omitted)

Wind speed
and direction
(21 to 25 mi per hr.)

Amount of
pressure change
last 3 hrs.
(tenths of millibars)

Temperature

56 ⊆ 247 +28
     •
9 --- 2 4.5

Barometric
tendency in past
3 hrs. (rising)

Amount of clouds
(sky 5/10 covered)

Weather- past
6 hrs. (rain)

Present weather
Rain and drizzle
(slight)

Cloud type
Low cloud

Heighth of
cloud base
(300-599 ft.)

Amount of
precipitation
last 6 hrs.

There are also *rain gauges* which collect and measure rainfall to a hundredth part of an inch, and *anemometers* whose hollow cups whirl in the wind and measure its speed, or velocity. To determine direction and speed of wind at high altitudes, gas-filled balloons are sent aloft. A theodolite, similar to a surveyor's instrument, is used to observe the balloons; radar follows them above clouds.

Some weather stations send up *radiosondes* twice daily. Instruments attached to a balloon radio back a record of pressure, temperature and humidity, until the lessened pressure of higher altitudes explodes the balloon and the instruments float down safely by parachute.

How is a weather map put together? Many people are needed to bring the daily weather maps to you on radio or television. Weather stations all over the world contribute information to our forecasting centers. Information comes in from airplanes in flight and ships at sea.

Every hour observations are taken at 400 stations along our nation's airways. More detailed observations are made every six hours. At almost the same instant, from Maine to California, more than 9,000 volunteers take observations and submit data on local weather to their nearest weather station.

The data collected is condensed and sent by telegraph to Suitland, Maryland, a few miles from Washington, D. C. Here is located the National Meteorological Center, headquarters of the United States Weather Forecasting System. Every six hours this weather center reports to more than 100 forecasting stations in major cities around the country. It gives a complete analysis of regional weather conditions. Each of the offices adapts these central reports to its own area. From here the information goes to the public through newspaper maps and television and radio broadcasts.

At Weather Bureau offices, maps are drawn four times a day. Maps of the upper level atmosphere are drawn twice a

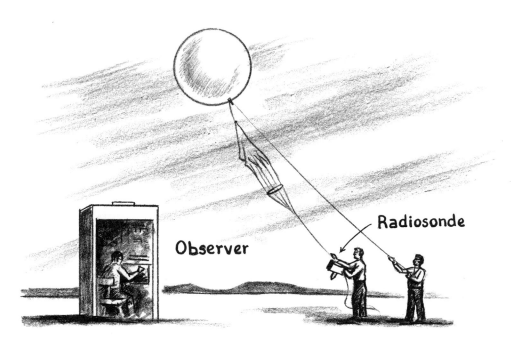

Radiosonde being released. Observer follows flight by radio.

day. Predictions are made from the information gathered and indicated on maps. Separate maps show differences in air pressure at various altitudes. Temperature charts are similar to maps with contour lines or isobars. In this case, lines of equal temperature are called *isotherms*. Winds aloft charts are also used in preparing forecasts.

Some forecasting is now done by machine. Electronic computers work out predictions and even print forecast maps.

The weatherman's maps, predictions and special reports are important to all of us. As a heavy snow storm moves across the eastern part of the country, it may dump ten inches of snow on New York City. Meteorologists, charting the course of the storm, predict the heavy snowfall and snow removal crews can prepare for it. While the snow is still falling, roads are being cleared and made safe for travel.

WEATHER MAP CODE FIGURES AND SYMBOLS

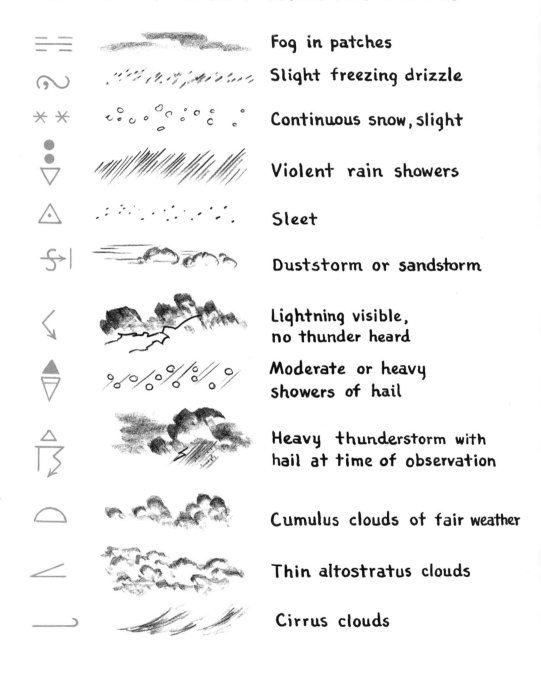

☰		Fog in patches
∿		Slight freezing drizzle
✳ ✳		Continuous snow, slight
▽		Violent rain showers
△		Sleet
⊸		Duststorm or sandstorm
↙		Lightning visible, no thunder heard
▲		Moderate or heavy showers of hail
⏚		Heavy thunderstorm with hail at time of observation
⌒		Cumulus clouds of fair weather
∠		Thin altostratus clouds
⌐		Cirrus clouds

Rains and melting snow may turn quiet rivers into raging floods in the Midwest. Hundreds of observers from the River and Flood Forecasting Service of the Weather Bureau report river stages and check rainfall. Flood forecasts and warnings are issued regularly for about 700 points on the principal rivers of the United States. When necessary, people and valuables can be moved to higher ground.

Frost warnings aid fruit growers. If a cold front is expected to drop temperatures below freezing, smudge pots can be lighted to prevent loss of crops. Warning facilities charts are issued by the Weather Bureau for coastal areas and the Great Lakes. These maps list offices giving twenty-four-hour telephone service for marine forecasts and small craft warnings, as well as broadcast schedules for radio and television stations giving warning reports. They include antenna locations of radio stations to aid boats having radio-direction-finding gear.

Our most dangerous storms swirl up out of the Caribbean. Before our hurricane warning system was begun in 1938, they struck with little advance warning. Many lives were lost. Today, as a hurricane moves in toward the coast, Army and Navy planes equipped with radar take turns diving through the center of the storm. They report its location and intensity. Automatic weather stations and radar installations along the coast record its progress.

At weather stations, the hurricane's position is marked on maps. Hourly bulletins are sent out. Each year the job of accurately mapping the paths of hurricanes and issuing storm warnings saves hundreds of lives and millions of dollars in property damage. If you wish to follow a hurricane and plot its course from weather bulletins, you may purchase a Hurricane Tracking Chart from the Superintendent of Documents, Washington, D. C., for ten cents.

Our major airports have weather stations to insure safe flying. Before each flight the pilot looks over the latest weather

71

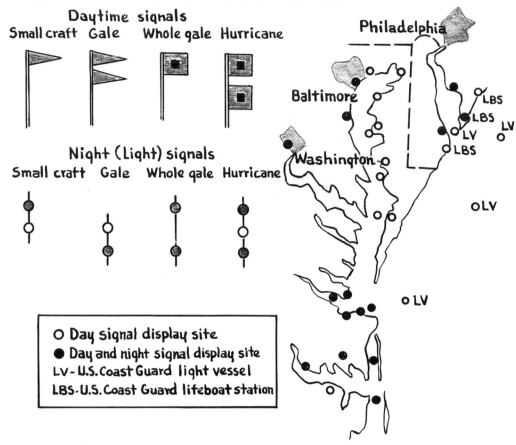

COASTAL WARNING FACILITIES CHART

Daytime signals
Small craft Gale Whole gale Hurricane

Philadelphia

Baltimore

Night (Light) signals
Small craft Gale Whole gale Hurricane

Washington

LBS
LBS
LV
LV
LBS

OLV

O LV

O Day signal display site
● Day and night signal display site
LV - U.S. Coast Guard light vessel
LBS - U.S. Coast Guard lifeboat station

maps. If the weather is bad, he may have to use an alternate route to get around a storm area. Once in the air, the pilot keeps a constant check on weather conditions, radioing back information. Forecasters rely heavily on reports from pilots as to turbulence and icing of aircraft.

Maps showing wind speeds and direction are important to forecasters and airplane navigators. Winds at lower levels blow at a reduced speed because of friction with the earth. Upper level maps show the paths of fast-moving jet streams of air which flow at 20,000 to 40,000 feet. Blowing along at speeds of 50 to 250 miles per hour, they give a lift to any plane that can "hitch a ride." Flights are planned to take advantage of these winds; less fuel is needed if winds help move the plane along.

In 1959, the U. S. Weather Bureau began a new high-altitude forecasting service to forecast flying weather up to 42,000 feet —nearly eight miles. Most of the necessary information is gathered by balloons released every six hours from seven main stations from Honolulu, Hawaii, and Anchorage, Alaska, to San Juan, Puerto Rico. Information is sent to Suitland where it is plotted on charts and sent to airports across the country.

Thus, we see how day-to-day weather affects our lives. But this is not the whole story. *Climate* determines how and where we live, what kind of houses we build, what we grow and what clothes we wear. Climate is the pattern of weather over the years. The Weather Bureau furnishes many climate maps covering a wide range of data.

Suppose you like winter sports. There are climate maps that show how many inches of snow to expect in the winter and how many days there will be snow on the ground in a particular area. Perhaps you are planning to move to a farm, or some-

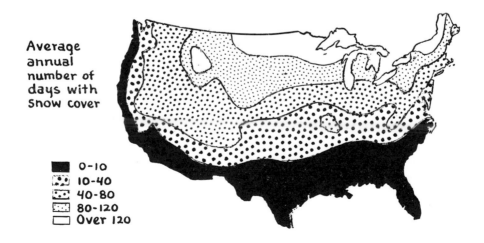

Average annual number of days with snow cover

0-10
10-40
40-80
80-120
Over 120

one in your family is interested in gardening. A climate map would tell you when to expect the first and last killing frost, or the average amount of rain that falls during the growing season.

The science of weather forecasting has advanced tremendously in recent years. The forecast record of the Weather Bureau is now more than 85 per cent accurate. Yet there is still much we need to know about the weather. Vast regions of the earth have few weather observations or none at all. We now observe only about 10 per cent of the earth's atmosphere through weather stations, balloons, planes and ships. Tiros I, our first weather satellite, was successfully fired into orbit in April, 1960, its television cameras taking pictures of the clouds over vast areas of the earth. Several such satellites will be able to cover the entire earth. They will enable the weatherman to observe the pattern of weather all over the globe at the same time. Satellite observations will help us to obtain data from polar regions, vast expanses of ocean and unexplored areas in Asia. This wealth of information will lead to greater accuracy in weather maps and the forecasts which follow.

8. Which Way Do We Go?

America has been called a "nation on wheels." It is estimated that by 1975 there will be 100 million motor vehicles in the United States. By then our new federal highway system should be complete — 40,000 miles of superhighways. As each new section is opened up, a new line is inked in on road maps of the area. The average road map has about 1,000 revisions each year.

Air travel is increasing also. New York City airports often handle 2,000 take-offs and landings in a single day. Pilots need maps for navigation, and air passengers are furnished maps to help them enjoy their flights.

And America is fast becoming a nation of boat enthusiasts. Boats of all types and sizes dot shores, rivers and lakes. There is plenty of room for travel by water; we have over 75,000 miles of coastline. The Mississippi River is the mainstream of a network of inland waterways more than 12,000 miles in length. This does not count the intercoastal waterways run-

A few typical
NAUTICAL SYMBOLS

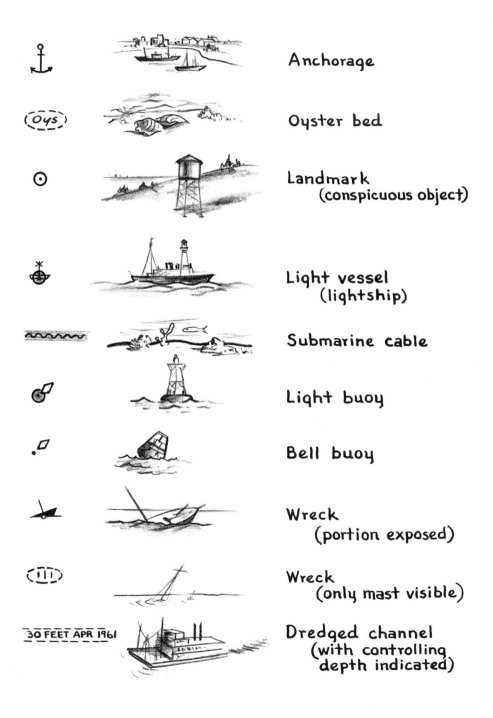

Anchorage

Oyster bed

Landmark
    (conspicuous object)

Light vessel
    (lightship)

Submarine cable

Light buoy

Bell buoy

Wreck
    (portion exposed)

Wreck
    (only mast visible)

Dredged channel
    (with controlling
      depth indicated)

ning nearly 2,000 miles through protected waters along our coasts. There are also thousands of lakes in the United States. All these areas of water need charting to make and keep them safe for navigation.

The *road map* is probably our most familiar map. Some of the best maps made by private companies are road maps, and nearly every filling station gives them away free of charge. Some oil companies operate touring services with routes marked and the maps bound in booklet form.

The first road map printed for the public was in *Tulley's Almanac* of 1698 published in Boston. It showed a list of towns, roads and distances from Boston. Before highways were numbered, road atlases used photographs of landmarks, turns and intersections to guide drivers. They were often more confusing than helpful.

Today's road map is usually very detailed and often colorful. The map contains a complete pattern of roads with their route numbers. Roads most often appear in red, black or blue, the red roads being the main highways and in the best condition. Cities and towns are indicated and mileage figures noted between principal points. An index is included. Such items as bridges, tolls and points of interest are usually shown. Through routes are often emphasized. Large-scale views show metropolitan areas and sometimes points of interest within, and easy routes through, cities. The latest changes in highways, detours and road conditions are included. Special maps are made for such toll roads as the Pennsylvania Turnpike or New York Thruway.

In our federal highway system, highways running east and west are even numbers, starting with low numbers in the North. U. S. 90 is the most southern route. Highways running north and south are uneven numbers. The lowest is Route 1 in the East. Route 101 runs along the West coast.

The new interstate network will reverse these patterns. Odd

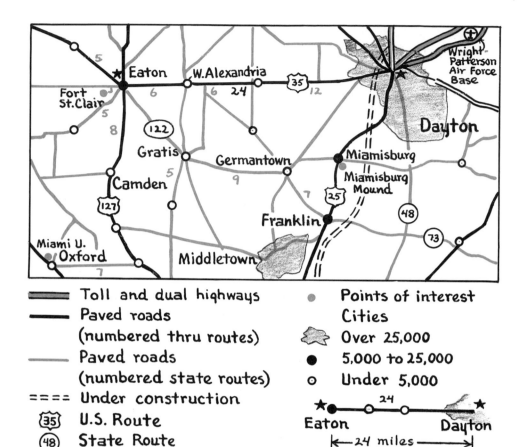

Toll and dual highways

Paved roads
(numbered thru routes)

Paved roads
(numbered state routes)

==== Under construction

35 U.S. Route

48 State Route

● Points of interest

Cities

Over 25,000

● 5,000 to 25,000

o Under 5,000

Eaton — 24 — Dayton

|← 24 miles →|

and even numbers will run in the same directions, but low numbers will be at the opposite side of the country. Route 5 will cut down the Pacific coast and Route 95, the Atlantic coast.

If you are going to travel by water, you will find an endless variety of nautical charts available for our coasts, rivers and lakes. Suppose you were sailing across Cape Cod Bay and into Plymouth Harbor. On your map depths are marked in numerous places. Your boat may be in waters twenty feet deep, while just beyond are depths of but a few feet. As you come into the harbor, you go between channel buoys that mark a safe passageway. On the chart, channels are shown in white and shallow waters in blue. Buoys are red on the right and black on the left. A symbol for a sunken ship is indicated, and off to your left you may see a bit of wreckage protruding from the water.

As you enter the harbor, you would switch to a large-scale chart of Plymouth harbor to find your way through the narrow channels to dock safely. If you should want additional data for these waters, you may find it in the Coast Pilot Guidebook for this section. A weekly notice to mariners adds any new data to the chart.

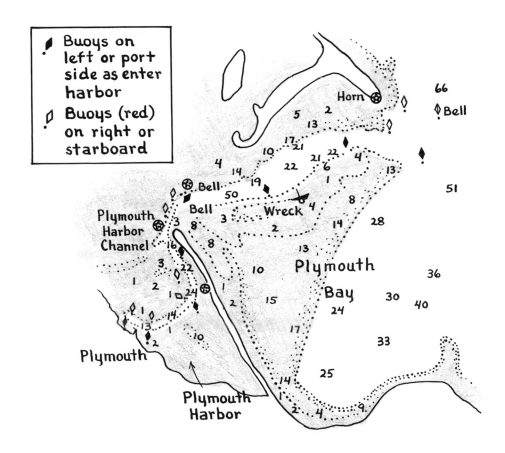

Navigation charts note the positions of lighthouses, light-ships and buoys which mark off safe channels and point out dangerous obstructions. Buoys are not only brightly painted, but are different shapes so that they may be easily identified in bad weather. Some have whistles or horns, others a steel clapper which clangs against a thousand-pound bell as the buoy rolls with the sea. A new type radar buoy has large fins to reflect a ship's signal.

Scales of nautical charts run from 1:2,200 to about 1:5,000,000. Index maps are available. Many areas overlap. The smallest scale nautical charts are *sailing charts*. These help the mariner fix his position as he nears the coast or sails between distant ports. This type of chart has a generalized shoreline. Only the principal outer lights, buoys and landmarks are shown.

General charts are for coastwise navigation *outside* outlying reefs and shoals.

Coast charts are for *inshore* navigation leading to large bays, harbors and inland waterways.

Harbor charts are large-scale. They cover harbors, anchor-age areas and small waterways.

Tidal current charts show direction and velocity of these currents. Tides go out and come in every six hours, reaching high and low tide an hour later each day. A series of twelve maps is included for each area, one for each hour of the tidal cycle. Many harbors have channels which are too shallow to use at low tide. Along open coasts, tides usually rise less than eight feet, but along funnel-shaped bays, such as the Bay of Fundy, they may rise as much as forty or fifty feet. The rise and fall of tides, direction and velocity of tidal current are recorded at many points. The data obtained is fed into a machine which predicts daily tides a year or more in advance.

Since 1841, the Great Lakes Survey has been charting the lakes with their 8,000 miles of shoreline. Large-scale *Great Lakes Charts* show depths in feet; small-scale ones often show

80

it in fathoms. (One fathom equals six feet.) On the back of the maps is an index and list of symbols. The charts are similar to coast and harbor charts.

Intercoastal waterway charts cover most of the area along our eastern and Gulf coasts from Boston to Brownsville, Texas. Natural waterways, rivers, creeks, inlets are mapped, as well as canals and dredged channels. Channel markers, day beacons and buoys are clearly marked. Marsh lands are shown in green. Clearance for bridges is specified, both for bridges when open and when closed.

If you should want to sail inland, connecting waterways that lead up the many rivers are also mapped. The Mississippi and its tributaries cover much of the interior of the country.

There were no buoys or lights on the Mississippi in Mark Twain's time. Pilots had to follow a constantly changing river, relying mainly on experience. The river is now kept under control with levees, dredged channels, and by-passes, all of which are marked on charts. Navigation markers include lights, day markers (large white diamond-shaped boards) and buoys. Two thousand lights hung on posts along the Mississippi and Ohio River systems mark the shorelines. But channels still change as sand and silt shift with the currents. River buoys need to be moved often; maps are soon outdated.

A folder of maps of the Mississippi River from Cairo, Illinois, to the Gulf of Mexico is published each year. The maps show channels, navigation lights, levees and sketches of locks and bridges. One large-scale map of the Mississippi is 48 feet long.

Would you like to walk the length of the Mississippi? You can do so in a very few minutes. There is a model map of the river at Clinton Waterways Experiment Station in Clinton, Mississippi. It is part of a flood control program of the U. S. Army Corps of Engineers. On the model it would take you five minutes to walk up the river from New Orleans to Pittsburgh where the Ohio River forms.

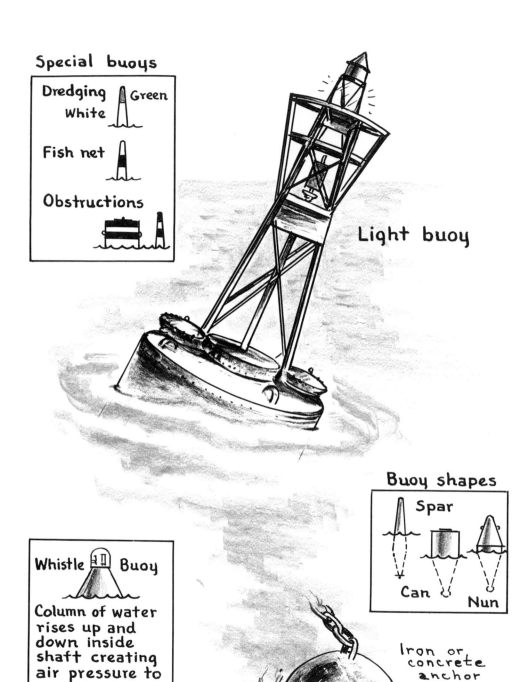

Special buoys

Dredging — Green / White

Fish net

Obstructions

Light buoy

Buoy shapes

Spar

Can

Nun

Whistle Buoy

Column of water rises up and down inside shaft creating air pressure to operate buoy

Iron or concrete anchor

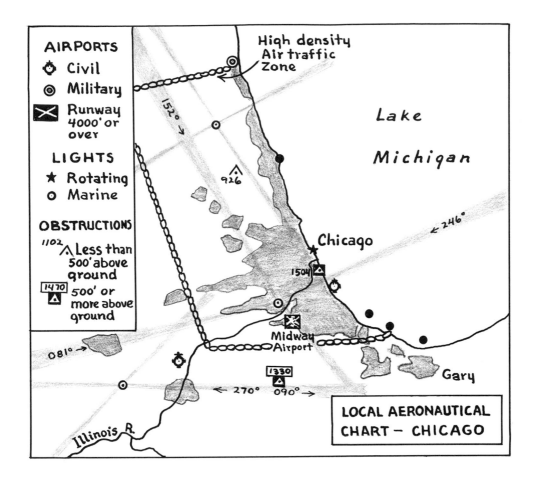

AIRPORTS
⚓ Civil
◉ Military
❌ Runway 4000' or over

LIGHTS
★ Rotating
○ Marine

OBSTRUCTIONS
1102 ⋀ Less than 500' above ground
1470 ⬛⧊ 500' or more above ground

High density Air traffic Zone

152°→

Lake Michigan

926

←246°

Chicago

1504

◀

081°→

◀

Midway Airport

1330

Gary

←270° 090°→

Illinois R.

LOCAL AERONAUTICAL
CHART — CHICAGO

Not everyone is interested in boats. Perhaps you will want to learn to pilot a plane. If you do, there are nearly a dozen types of aeronautical maps available. Some are for slow-flying planes, others for fast jets and several for individual airports. Scales for aeronautical maps vary from 1:5,000,000 to 1:12,000.

Most aeronautical charts have a great deal of additional data printed on the back of the map. All would contain such aeronautical symbols as airports, navigation lights, radio facilities and topographic symbols.

All such charts show radio range stations, marked by over-lapping crosses. The size of the cross indicates the power of the station. Each sends out four beams, which intersect beams from other stations to form an aerial highway system. Points of intersection give a "fix," or check point. Towers are placed two miles or more from the airport they serve to keep them from being a flight hazard.

Radio Facility Charts give detailed information on radio stations. Maps of two adjoining areas are printed on either side. A list of all stations and their frequencies is included with the maps.

U. S. Air Force *Global Navigation and Planning Charts* cover large sections of the world on a single sheet. Thirteen such sheets cover most of the northern hemisphere. Maps are printed in shaded relief, valleys and level areas are green, hills and mountains yellow, glaciers and pack ice white. Only the larger airports are shown. The letter J above the runway pattern means jet facilities are available.

Route charts provide information for long range, high altitude, high speed navigation. *Jet navigation charts* show degrees of latitude and longitude, and are used for plotting lines of position.

World Aeronautical Charts provide a standard series of charts for overland navigation by moderate-speed aircraft. *Sectional charts* are designed for contact flying — navigating by visible landmarks on the ground — by slow or moderate-speed planes.

If you were forced down while flying with a sectional chart, you could look on the back of the chart and find, along with other data, diagrams of visual emergency signals. If a member of the party is injured, you would know that a straight line marked out with stones or cloth means "requires doctor, serious injuries." Or if you are lost in the wilderness, you might mark off a square, meaning "require map and compass."

84

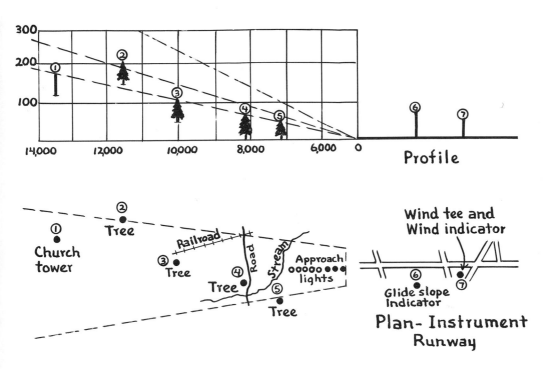

300
200
100

14,000　　12,000　　10,000　　8,000　　6,000　　0　　Profile

Church tower ①
② Tree
③ Tree
④ Tree
⑤ Tree
Railroad
Road
Stream
Approach lights
ooooo ●●●

Wind tee and Wind indicator

⑥
⑦
Glide slope Indicator

Plan- Instrument Runway

Obstruction chart, Teterboro Airport, New Jersey

Local charts for pilots are large-scale charts of highly congested metropolitan areas, also used for visual navigation. Both sectional and local charts list airports on the back. Elevation, latitude and longitude, number of runways, their surface, length of longest runway, lighting are noted here.

Air space is getting crowded. "Stacking," or circling while awaiting permission to land, is often necessary. Two special charts for aid in approach and landing at airports are *obstruction charts* and *instrument approach and landing charts*. The latter are made up of several very small maps, only 5 by 8 inches, showing different systems of instrument landing. One small sketch shows the airport buildings and pattern of runways. A larger map takes in the surrounding area and gives the approach patterns and the proper turns to make if the approach misses. Obstruction charts are much larger and show,

85

in detailed maps and side elevations, obstructions on and surrounding the airport.

People travel more miles by plane than by train, excluding commuters in large cities. Each airline offers some type of *air route map* for their passengers. Often they are in full color in booklet form, with historic facts and pictorial drawings included.

Railroad maps are less decorative and usually simplify and distort areas to show principal routes larger so that the many stations may be included. Maps are usually included with timetables.

There are even maps for those who like to walk. The *New York Walk Book* maps trails and topography and describes geology, trees and plants. As you can see, maps are needed wherever and however we travel.

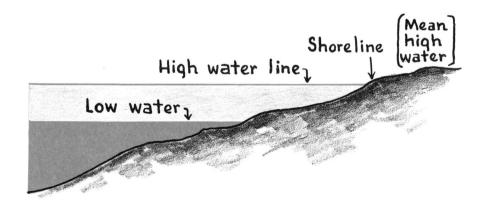

9.   Through a Magnifying Glass

With the aid of large-scale maps we can look at the earth closely, as through a magnifying glass. We can see roads, lanes and small creeks, houses and lot lines. Our "magnifying glass" will even penetrate the earth so that we can see rock formations or utility lines under a city's streets. Topographic and nautical maps are probably the most important large-scale maps — which are the kind that show the greatest detail — but there are many other types available.

Every ten years our government prepares a "magnifying glass" through which we can take a close look at ourselves. It is called the census. *Census maps* cover every dwelling in the United States. Special maps are made up dividing the country into 250,000 districts; a separate map is prepared for each district. Some cover hundreds of square miles in desolate areas. Others may be but a single apartment house. Maps are based on aerial photographs, building plans and surveyors' charts.

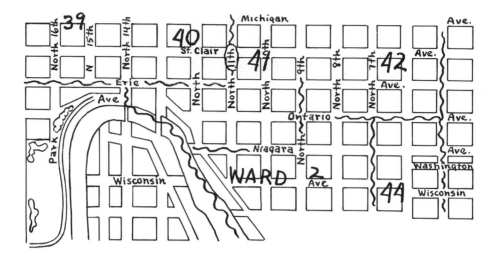

Census figures are of great help to legislators in determining employment, housing and health conditions. Over 60 questions were included in the 1960 census, and the information is being used in the preparation of 350,000 maps which are of great value to government agencies, business, and city or township planning boards. The first census in 1790 provided for a nationwide count to keep state representation in Congress up-to-date.

City maps are published by the government and also by private publishers as street guides. Large-scale maps show every building; smaller-scale ones, only city blocks. Some may show only patterns of residential, park, commercial, industrial and agricultural areas. Streets are often drawn wider than they really are to permit labeling. Such maps often have a street index included.

Some eighty detailed city maps have been published by the Geological Survey. They include topographic features, streets, buildings and woodland areas. A whole city can be photographed from the air in an hour or two. It would be impossible to keep our rapidly growing cities up-to-date without aerial mapping.

Zoning maps are carefully worked out in detail, not only for today, but in terms of future growth of homes and industry. They help cities and suburban areas to obtain an orderly growth.

Detailed *business or commercial maps* are mounted to receive colored push pins. Salesmen or work crews may be easily located on these maps and territories marked off. Truck owners use such maps to locate the quickest and best routes for transporting goods.

Real estate or insurance maps need to be large-scale and to contain very specific information. The electric company in Philadelphia uses a map made from a huge photographic map about 33 x 45 feet in size. Each section was made from dozens of aerial photographs carefully assembled into a photo-mosaic and then re-photographed.

Fire and mortgage underwriters need maps to show street widths, lot lines, structures, materials used in walls and wiring. Such *insurance maps* are made with a scale of one inch to 50 or 100 feet. Charts are often hand-colored. It takes an atlas of about 40 volumes to cover New York City in such detail.

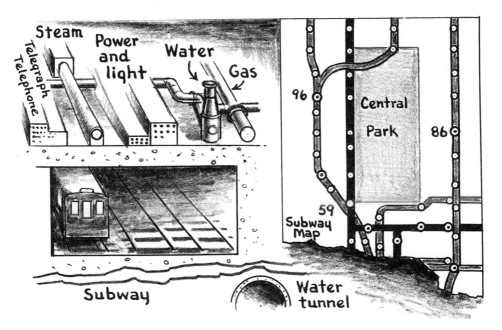

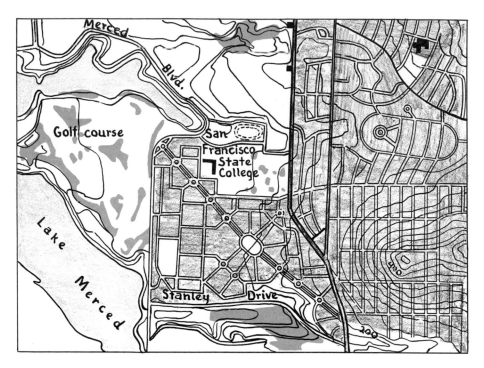

Section of San Francisco and vicinity

It is not enough to map every street, property line and building in our cities and towns. Beneath our cities lie mazes of wires and tubes. In New York City a billion gallons of water flow each day through between 5,000 and 6,000 miles of tunnels. Five thousand miles of sewers carry it away. Steam lines, gas mains, television cables, and electrical cables all crisscross under the busy city. Fifteen million miles of telephone cable serve the city. Without maps of this underground network, it would be almost impossible to locate and repair broken mains and cables.

The earth and the structure of rocks beneath it are the source of many detailed maps. *Geologic maps* are based on topographic maps which show physical features of the land above ground. Bedrock information or other facts about the area below ground are printed over in colors.

90

The Bureau of Chemistry and Soils issues colored maps called *soil maps*. They usually cover a county, are also drawn on topographic base maps, and provide information about the soil in that particular section.

The United States Department of Agriculture issues *soil conservation maps* which show conditions of the land. The maps are broken down into various classifications — land suitable for cultivation, land suitable for limited cultivation and land not suited for cultivation. Different colors represent various areas and are printed over a mosaic map made from aerial photographs.

Geologists use an airborne *magnetometer* to locate iron ore deposits, various other metals and potential oil sites. Maps are then made of what resources lie beneath the ground. In a few years as much data has been supplied by this method as might have been gathered in a century by ground search.

One of the best mapped areas in the world is the British Isles. *British ordnance maps* are the official government maps

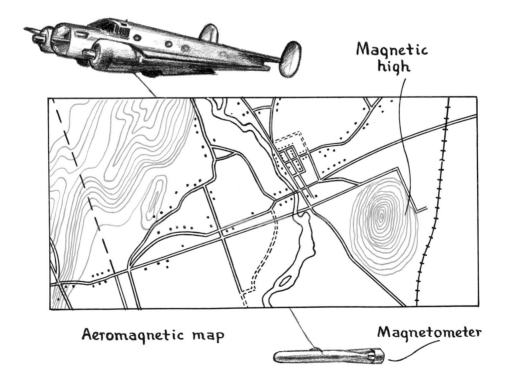

Magnetic high

Aeromagnetic map

Magnetometer

based on a system of imaginary squares covering all of England and Scotland. The maps appear in different scales. Every house, garden and footpath is shown on the larger-scale maps, prepared in a scale of six inches to the mile. *Land-use maps* of Britain have been made, using the ordnance maps as a base. They are at a scale of 1:63,360 — one inch to a mile. Every field in Great Britain has been marked on these maps with labels or letters to indicate grass, forest, orchards.

Large-scale maps serve our armed forces during war time. *Target charts* cover a single city, bridge, factory or other target. Only those features such as railroads, roads, water areas and other landmarks needed to locate the target are placed on the map. The target is indicated by concentric circles like those on an archery target.

Landing maps for troops are very detailed. Those taking part in the landing operations need to know tide levels, topography of the beach and the land beyond and the kind of bottom. The landing area or beach area is at the top of the map, no matter what its true direction, so that the region is readily viewed as it will be by oncoming assault troops.

Several very unusual maps were made during World War II. Pilots carried small maps printed on nylon and folded like handkerchiefs to fit in their pockets. If a pilot were forced down, salt water would not affect the map. On night flights, pilots had maps printed in fluorescent ink which could be read under ultraviolet light. The pilot switched on a small lamp on his helmet to read his map. No one at a distance could see the light.

Large-scale maps are quickly outdated. Many areas that show little or no change on a small-scale map will show tremendous changes when a small section is mapped in detail.

10. A Long Look at the World

After looking at the world through the magnifying glass of large-scale maps, suppose we pull back and take a long look at the earth. Small-scale maps show us our world as it would appear from a great distance.

There has long been a need for a small-scale map of the world with each sheet in the same scale yet large enough to show a good bit of detail. In 1891, an International Map of the World was proposed, at a scale of 1 to 1,000,000. It was begun in the early twentieth century. Most sheets cover 6° north and south and 4° east and west. When complete it was to contain 1,500 sheets, but only about 400 had been published by World War II. The entire set has been superceded by the 1:1,000,000 maps of the Army Map Service and the United States Coast and Geodetic Survey which now cover most of the world. The

WORLD 1:1,000,000 (EUROPE)

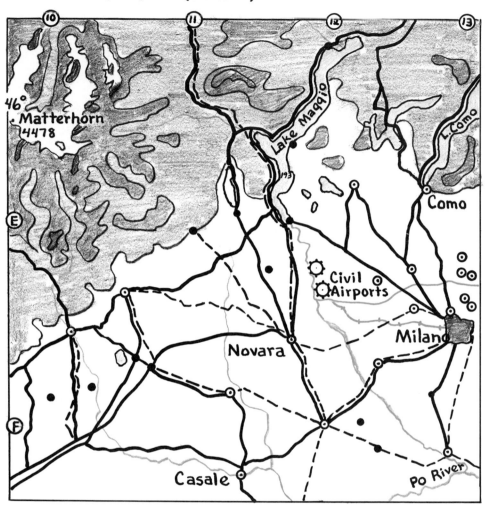

Population
   Above 100,000
   10,000 to 100,000
   Under 10,000
Roads
Railroads
Major Civil Airports

Spot heighths
(in metres)   1243.
Lake levels   193
Glaciers
Irrigation canal
Marsh, swamp
Water conduits

Section of International Map of the World

Army Map Service of the Corps of Engineers has the responsibility of providing accurate maps of every land area in the world where the United States may have to fight. With the help of nearly fifty friendly nations, the AMS is at work to reach this goal.

Many other types of maps give us a long look at the world. We see continents spread before us in *landscape maps* which reveal the natural coloring of their vegetation. All areas of the earth are usually pictured as though seen in summer. The dark green of evergreen forests are contrasted with the tan of sandy deserts. Ice and snow, glaciers and ice caps, colorless tundra and bare mountain slopes add to this picture of the earth.

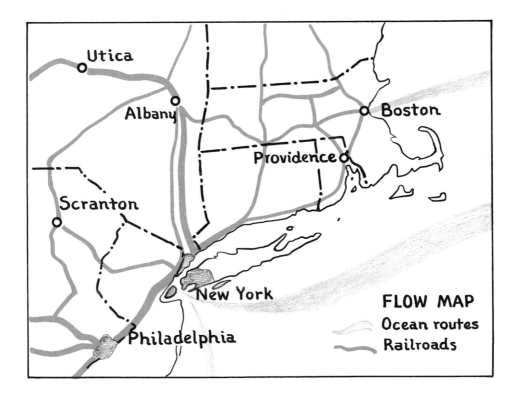

FLOW MAP
Ocean routes
Railroads

Land-use maps show the uses the land is being put to. Large-scale British land-use maps mentioned in the previous chapter can be the basis of small-scale land-use maps. Unfortunately most of the world is not mapped in this way. If it were, these maps would help people use their land to the best possible advantage.

If these land-use maps show only a single product or a group of related products, they are called *economic maps. Distribution maps* show areas of population, rainfall, religion, or any of numerous other subjects. Economic and distribution maps of the world are often used by the Department of State. You are probably familiar with these maps from your atlas or textbooks.

A map which shows movement is called a *flow map.* It can show anything from ocean trade routes to the westward movement of the center of our population. For example, on a traffic flow map, the thickness of the lines shows the relative amount of travel on each railroad or ocean shipping line.

Pictorial or decorative maps can and have been made on nearly every subject. In some cases, pictures block out so much of the map that the map itself becomes secondary. Decorative mural maps are made in very large sizes and of many materials. Some are made of mosaic or cut in stone and have insets of brass, copper or enamel.

Pictorial maps showing battles or war strategy often combine the flow map with the pictorial. Many of these maps were made in World War II and in the Korean War to show movements of troops. Broad arrows and symbols represented tanks, planes and ships.

There are many imaginary lines and divisions used in map-making. Along with contour lines and latitude and longitude is another type of imaginary line marking the boundaries between countries, states or local areas — the political boundary. With the gradual exploration and settlement of America it was necessary to set up ways of distributing land. In New

American attack on Luzon, World War II

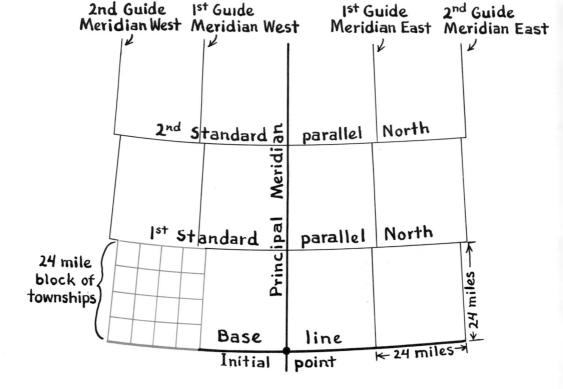

2nd Guide Meridian West 1st Guide Meridian West   1st Guide Meridian East   2nd Guide Meridian East

2nd Standard parallel North

1st Standard parallel North

Principal Meridian

24 mile block of townships

Base line
Initial point

← 24 miles →
← 24 miles →

Public land survey divides public lands

England it became the custom for the legislature to grant a group of individuals a *township* of land which they undertook to settle. They mapped the township, dividing it into village lots, fields, woods and common pasture.

When the original thirteen states were admitted to the Union, they retained management of the ungranted land within their boundaries. Vermont, Kentucky, Tennessee, Texas, Maine and West Virginia also retained their land. The government owned nearly all the land in the remaining twenty-nine states. This land system made possible rapid settlement of our country, from the Appalachians to the Pacific, in little more than a century.

1st Standard parallel North

| Township 4 North Range line 4 West | T 4 N R 3 W | T 4 N R 2 W | ←less than→ 6 miles |

Township line

T 3 N

R 4 W

2nd Guide Meridian West

1st Guide Meridian West

Range line

1 mile

6	5	4	3	2	1
7	8	9	10	11	12
18	17	16	15	14	13
19	20	21	22	23	24
30	29	28	27	26	25
31	32	33	34	35	36

1 mile

Base line

←6 miles→

←6 miles→

A 24-mile block of townships. Each is subdivided into sections.

The General Land Office is the U. S. Government's oldest surveying and mapping bureau. About two-thirds of our country, thirty states in all (including Alaska), have been covered by the great public land surveys which opened up the West. The survey is a rectangular system used by the Federal government to divide public lands.

All public land surveys in a given area are mapped in reference to two lines — a *principal meridian* (a true north-south line) and a *base line* (a true east-west line, or parallel). There are thirty-four different systems in the United States and Alaska, each with its own principal meridian and base line. Parallel to the base line are *standard parallels,* located 24 miles

99

apart, north and south of the base line. From the base line and each standard parallel, guide meridians are run due north ending at the next standard parallel. They are also spaced 24 miles apart, east and west of the principal meridian.

Each area of approximately 24 miles each way is further divided into 16 parts. Each of these parts is six miles north and south and approximately six miles east and west. These divisions are called *townships*, although they have no relationship to the townships of New England and elsewhere which are governing units.

Each township is subdivided into 36 *sections*, each approximately one mile square. Each section may be divided into *quarter sections* of 160 acres each. This is the size of a typical midwest farm.

This township and section system influenced the pattern of our country. It started the north-south and east-west pattern of roads, streets and houses. Many boundaries follow these parallels and meridians, and the regular pattern becomes readily apparent as you fly over the Midwest. The blocks of land are easily recognized from the air. Pilots of private planes often follow section lines as navigation guides.

Special maps mark our international boundaries. Many show the locations of boundary monuments which, in some places, are but a mile apart. There are several kinds of monuments used. One of the most common is five feet high and shaped like a miniature Washington Monument.

These boundary markers are a part of the history of our growing nation. One marker, a lead tablet, marked the French claim to the Ohio country in the year 1749. Another monument, called the Fairfax Stone, marked the western limits of Lord Fairfax's 5,000,000-acre land grant of two centuries ago in what is now Virginia. The state boundaries of Maryland, Virginia and West Virginia are based on such markers. A cast-iron boundary marker marked the line between Manitoba,

100

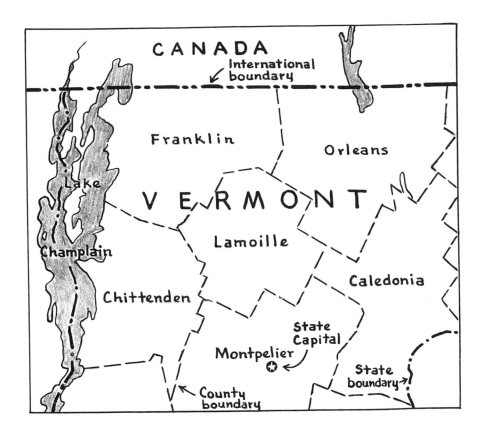

Canada, and the angle where our northern border juts up at
Lake of the Woods. It was not until 1925 that Canada and
the United States agreed on this point, settling a boundary
problem which had existed since the Revolutionary War.

Our boundaries, both state and national, have been subject to constant change. Many lines have been proposed and
finally settled after years of negotiation. These changes are
recorded on *political maps,* one of our most familiar maps,
showing the outlines of states or countries.

Some of the finest maps are produced by the National Geographic Society. Up-to-date, they show current changes in
the status of the world. In the decade between 1950 and 1960,

many new nations appeared, in Asia — Indonesia, Cambodia, North and South Vietnam and the United Arab Republic. The greatest change, of course, took place in Africa, with over half of the African countries becoming independent nations.

Boundaries have been changed as the result of both world wars. As world interest changes, new areas receive special attention. During World War II, such places as Iwo Jima and Bataan were prominently noted on maps and globes; Cape Canaveral has, in recent years, become of great interest. New maps feature places perhaps little known before.

A new look in international boundaries is taking place at the South Pole. An international treaty leaves the area open to all for exploration and use. It applies to all areas, except the high seas, below 60° south, taking in a region 4,000 miles across. This agreement is being studied as a model for the moon and the rest of the solar system. All such changes need to be recorded by cartographers.

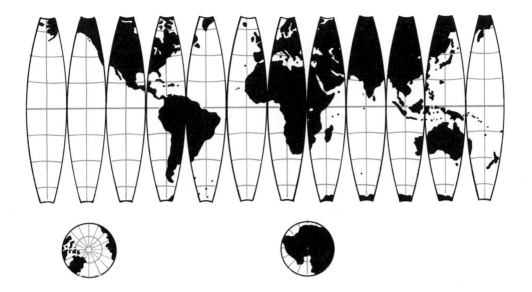

II.   How to Flatten a Round World

If the earth were flat, as some people thought in the time of Columbus, how much easier the job of map-making would be!

The globe is the only true picture of the earth. If you want to flatten out a globe, you have to crush it, tear it or stretch it — something has to give. Every flat map is a distortion of the globe.

The first globe of the earth that has survived was made by Martin Behaim, a German geographer, in the year Columbus discovered America. In the Age of Discovery that followed, the globe was ideal for showing the new geography. Many fine ones were made, some quite ornate.

Globes are made of many materials: spun aluminum, glass, wood fiber, plastic or cardboard pressed into molds. Others made of thin plastic can be inflated as easily as a toy balloon.

103

The map which is made to be pasted on the globe is made up of either 12 or 24 gores, as shown in the drawing here. Smaller globes are usually 12 gores, with the Arctic and Antarctic regions pasted on separately. We know that a flat piece of paper cannot be made to fit over a globe. But a narrow strip of paper fastened to the globe when wet will stretch enough to allow an almost perfect fit. The meridians must, of course, be the same length when on the globe, so the central meridian of each gore is drawn shorter than the two outside meridians. In adapting the gore to the globe, this central meridian is stretched.

Globes usually turn on an axis which is attached to a meridian ring. Some are placed in a cradle. You can pick up this kind and turn it in your hands like a ball. Some globes have a time dial placed over the North Pole axis. The time dial is divided into 24 parts, one for each hour of the day. This type of globe best illustrates ideas of time zones, day and night, summer and winter.

One of the finest globes in the world is located at Babson Institute, Wellesley Hills, Massachusetts. It is a revolving globe, 28 feet in diameter, and is made of porcelain enamel on steel. A globe that would fit in your pocket — not much larger than a golf ball — can be made also. But it would be of little use as a map. If you were interested in the road system of New Jersey, you would be out of luck, for the whole state of New Jersey would be barely visible. In order to have a ball of sufficient size to show this road pattern, you would need a globe of perhaps 100 feet in diameter — an awkward thing to carry along on a vacation trip!

Thus, while globes are the most accurate maps of the world, they are usually not the most convenient. A flat map is the only practical solution.

How do we perform this miracle of making a round surface flat? The key to this is our system of parallels and meridians,

104

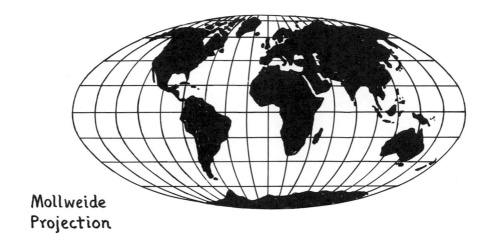

Mollweide
Projection

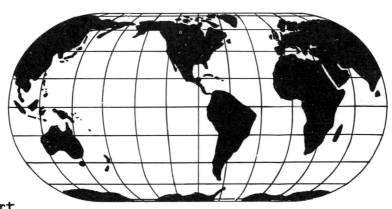

Eckert

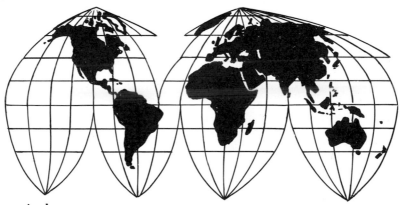

Interrupted

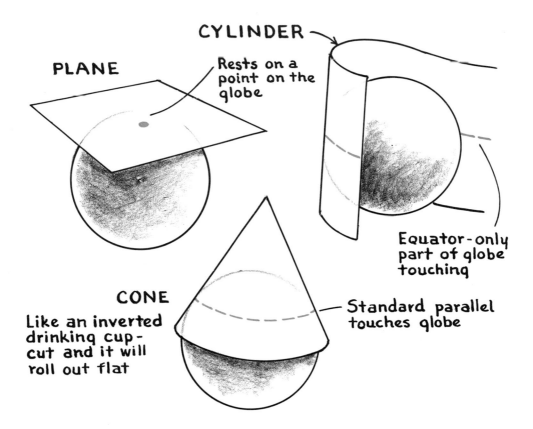

PLANE

CYLINDER

Rests on a point on the globe

Equator-only part of globe touching

CONE

Like an inverted drinking cup - cut and it will roll out flat

Standard parallel touches globe

which form a skeleton for our maps. Using them, we know that one thing will be correct on every map — each place on the map will be in its true location, in its proper relationship to the pattern of parallels and meridians. It will always be at the same latitude and longitude.

The precise distance or direction between these locations, the shape, or the area may be incorrect. Each flat map must lie a little. A round map cannot be straightened out without distortion of some sort. What a cartographer must do is decide the purpose of the map and then use or devise a *projection*, which will be accurate in terms of the purpose of the map.

Most map projections are related to a cylinder, cone or plane surface. Let us take a look at how a globe is projected. If we take a transparent globe with a light in the center, we can project the map onto a sheet of paper as a picture is projected on a screen. The paper may then be rolled into a cylinder, or a cone or remain level, as a plane. Now, after we project the globe onto one of these areas, each can be unrolled again as a flat map. This seemingly simple method is behind most map projections, but most need to be modified and are the result of complicated mathematical computations based on these visual methods. A recent National Geographic map of Asia was based on over 500 difficult computations in spherical trigonometry.

Aside from location, maps are concerned with shape, area, distance and direction. When the *shape* of small areas such as bays, lakes or islands is correct throughout the map, we call that map *conformal*. The scale changes over the map, but remains the same within any small area formed by meridians and parallels.

The *Lambert Conformal Conic* has two standard parallels. It is the most common projection for air navigation charts. The map is a compromise. The scale is nearly right; shape and area are close to being accurate.

When a map is *equal-area*, it simply means that you can place your finger, or anything else of a fixed size, any place on the map and in each case it will cover an area represent-

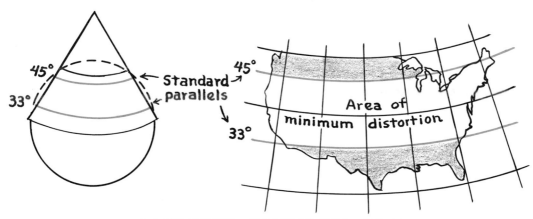

LAMBERT'S CONFORMAL CONIC

Every point on map shows
true distance and right
direction from center

ing the same amount of ground. Areas are equal, but are pulled out of shape so are not conformal. Each square between the same parallels has the same area as on the globe, but meridians do not cross at right angles. This distortion squeezes shapes near the edges. The Mollweide and Eckert projections are equal-area projections.

When all points on a map are in their true *direction* from the center of the map, we call it an *azimuthal* projection. Azimuth is another name for "bearing," the nautical word used for direction measured by the compass. Azimuthal Equidistant Projections — the full name for such maps — are drawn so that straight lines radiating from a central point to any other point represent the shortest distance (that is, an arc of a great circle) and the true direction. Azimuthal projections have many uses. From the central point on the map, distances and directions can be read quickly and easily for flying or navigation. Radio broadcasting beams can also be centered on the station from which they radiate. It is excellent for polar maps.

A projection can be centered upon any point of the globe. A *polar* projection is one which is centered upon either the

108

North or South Pole. Projections centered on a point along the equator are called *meridional*. Projections centered on neither the polar axis nor the equator are *transverse* or *oblique*, and are the most difficult to construct.

When a projection is cut apart and the large land masses separated, it is called an *interrupted projection*. There is less distortion near the edges, but ocean areas are hard to visualize because they are pulled apart.

The choice of the kind of projection becomes most important on world or hemisphere maps. It is here that distortions are greatest. The smaller the area to be included on a map, the more accurate it can be in shape, area, distance and direction. This is because any one square mile on the earth is relatively flat. It is when we take a larger portion of the globe that we get an increasing roundness and thus an increasing distortion when the area is flattened.

On world maps, only a few lines are in scale or exactly the same length as on a globe. All other lines are too long or too short. The only way to be accurate is to specify those lines that are true to scale. Sometimes the amount of error in other lines is indicated.

Perhaps the best known and the most criticized projection is the *Mercator*. It was designed in 1569 by the famous Flemish map-maker whose name it bears. Mercator balanced the stretched-out latitude and longitude to make it conformal — the shapes of small areas conforming to those on a globe. Large areas, however, become greatly distorted in size. This is no fault of the map for, as we have previously noted, no map can do everything. The Mercator does what it was intended to do. It is the only system which shows all compass directions as straight lines. Most navigation charts are of this projection. Its straight parallels mean that places of the same latitude are at the same height on the map. This helps in comparing climate, land-use and vegetation in various areas of the world also.

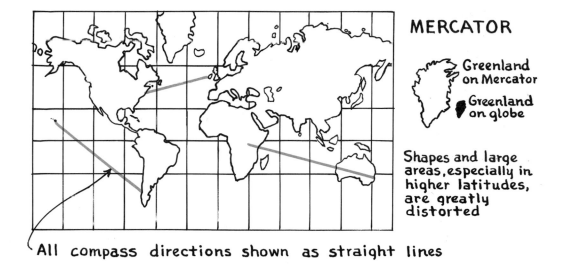

MERCATOR

Greenland
on Mercator

Greenland
on globe

Shapes and large
areas, especially in
higher latitudes,
are greatly
distorted

All compass directions shown as straight lines

The *orthographic* and *stereographic* projections were orig-
inated by Hipparchus in the second century B. C. The distortions of the orthographic are probably the most natural to
us, as they are just as they would be in a photograph of the
earth. We are used to seeing long rows of telephone poles grow
smaller in the distance.

The stereographic shows a complete hemisphere. A modified stereographic is being used in the first topographic map
of the moon's surface.

110

ORTHOGRAPHIC

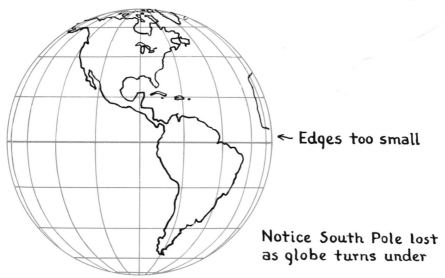

← Edges too small

Notice South Pole lost
as globe turns under

STEREOGRAPHIC

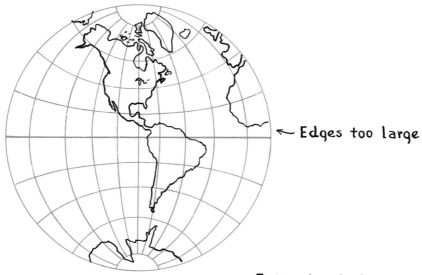

← Edges too large

Entire hemisphere
shown clearly here

12. Our World in Space

Before man actually travels out into space there are many things he needs to know. For many years the moon has been clearly seen through telescopes, photographed and carefully mapped. Other planets will also be viewed by television cameras from satellites and mapped before man attempts to explore them. Space adventurers will carry good maps along when they set out to explore these new worlds.

When we start talking about space mapping, such words as "fabulous" and "colossal" seem hardly adequate to describe the subject. A few figures will show the tremendous areas to be covered by our space maps. Picture yourself driving a car at 70 miles per hour on a roadway to the moon. If you drove without stopping, it would take over four months to reach the moon — and over *150 years* to reach the sun. Yet the next nearest star is nearly 300,000 times farther out in space than the sun, so far that distances to it and other stars are usually measured in light years. Light travels at 186,000 miles per second. If we could travel at this fantastic speed it would still take us over four years to reach that next nearest star and thousands or even millions of years to reach other stars. Even so, our most powerful telescopes cannot find an end to the universe.

Although we can see only about 2,000 stars on a clear night, there are millions or even billions of stars in a single galaxy or group of stars. Millions of galaxies fill the sky.

Stars seem stationary, but are moving at many miles per second in different directions deep in space, which makes the job of charting their position even more difficult.

Celestial globes have been used since the time of the Romans. They help us to understand the stars and their positions. Such globes of the heavens can be turned so that an imaginary line from the center of the globe passes through a star on the globe and if carried out into space would point to the same star in space.

One of the easiest ways to learn the positions of the stars is through constellations. These are imaginary forms given to groups of stars. Some constellations have been known for thousands of years. Look closely and — with a little imagination — you can see a bear, dragon, scorpion and winged horse. Of

Jodrell Bank
radiotelescope

Reflector bowl
250' in diameter

Star chart of autumn and winter

course, the best-known constellations are the Big and Little Dipper. *Star charts* are maps of these constellations.

Men have been studying the heavens through telescopes since Galileo first looked into space in 1609. The largest telescope in the world today is the 200-inch Hale Reflector at Palomar Observatory in California. With it, astronomers can photograph galaxies two billion light years away. Two instruments aid the telescope in gathering information — the camera and *spectroscope*. A special kind of reflector telescope, the Schmidt, allows rapid photographing of large areas of the sky. The spectroscope enables astronomers to break up starlight into separate

114

colors. By the shifting bands of color, astronomers can tell many things — a star's temperature and its physical make-up.

More recently developed are *radio telescopes*, whose huge dish-shaped disks reflect radio waves. Electrical forces in space send signals which give astronomers much information they cannot obtain with optical telescopes. Areas of the sky that seem empty to even the most powerful telescope and that record nothing on sensitive cameras are mapped with the radio telescope.

The new radio telescope now under construction in the mountains of West Virginia will be the largest in existence, its reflector 600 feet across. Its range in space is expected to be 19 times that of the Palomar telescope.

Another means to help astronomers solve the problems of mapping space is the *electronic computer*. Now an almost unlimited range of astronomical calculations can be solved in a fraction of the time it formerly took.

As seen from the earth, by far the most impressive object in space is our moon. Moon maps were drawn soon after the telescope was invented. In 1647, Hevelius of Danzig named 250 of the moon's features. Then in 1651, Riccioli published

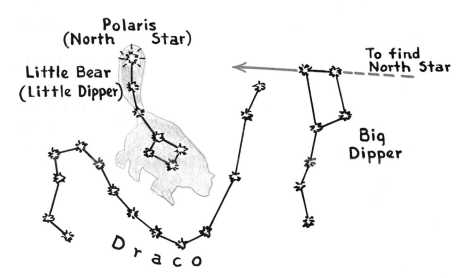

a map of the moon in which he named craters after famous philosophers of ancient Greece. Plains were called Maria (plural) or Mare (singular), the Latin word for seas, which they were at first thought to be. Sharp, jagged, lunar mountains throw clear shadows which help astronomers measure their heights. The highest peaks on the moon rise far above Mount Everest, earth's highest mountain.

Many thousands of photographs have been taken of the moon. About 30,000 craters have been mapped so far, but only about one crater in fifty is officially named. There are several types of craters. The largest in area are really slightly depressed plains, surrounded by mountains, and about 60 to 150 miles wide. Deeper craters are usually round and from 10 to 60 miles across. They also have mountains around them. Many contain peaks that rise up from the center of the crater floor.

In 1959, the Russian Lunik III satellite photographed and transmitted pictures of the far side of the moon for the first time. It marked the beginning of man's ability to send satellites into orbit around celestial bodies, photograph and map them.

The newest studies and resulting maps of the moon have been made for the purpose of providing information about its surface so that landing sites may be selected for spacecraft. The maps will also help in designing a vehicle to travel on the moon, once man has reached it.

Three map diagrams of the moon have been made by the Geological Survey for the Army engineers. The diameter of each is 36 inches. All show the part of the moon visible to us.

The first map diagram shows the physical features of the moon and the main surface regions of the moon. The second is a photographic map which has a graduated scale to allow for the curvature of the moon. The third diagram shows lunar rays, streaks across the moon's surface, some of which radiate hundreds of miles out from the craters where they seem to originate.

116

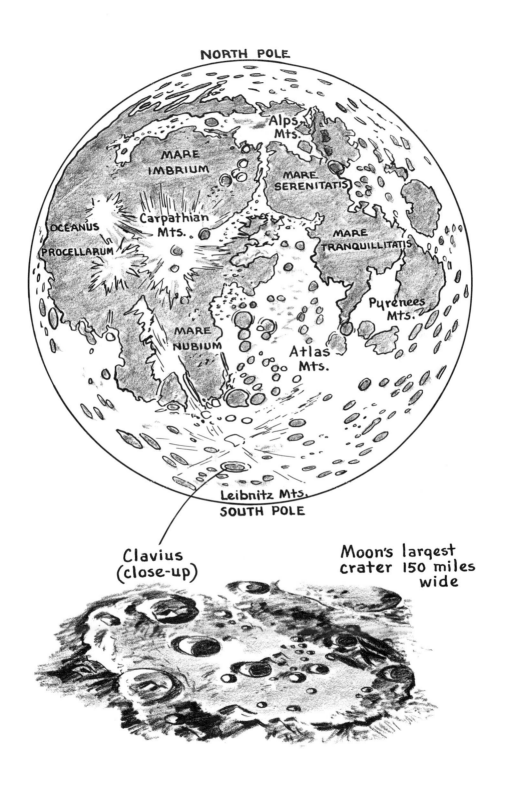

NORTH POLE

Alps Mts.

MARE IMBRIUM

MARE SERENITATIS

OCEANUS PROCELLARUM

Carpathian Mts.

MARE TRANQUILLITATIS

MARE NUBIUM

Pyrenees Mts.

Atlas Mts.

Leibnitz Mts.
SOUTH POLE

Clavius (close-up)

Moon's largest crater 150 miles wide

The Air Force is also completing a map of the moon. This contour map will be published in 84 sections at a scale of 16 miles to an inch. Fifteen thousand closeup photographs were taken of the moon through a 24-inch telescope. They were taken at different times, with changing shadows, and make it possible to measure accurately and map the contours of the areas photographed.

Next to the moon in interest are the planets which circle the sun. Mercury is the smallest planet. It has only hazy markings, and its surface is still a mystery. Venus has a dense atmosphere which conceals the planet's surface. Mars has two small moons and its surface can be studied through telescopes. Jupiter is the largest planet. It has twelve moons, Four are about the size of our moon and can easily be seen with field glasses. At least 2,000 small *asteroids* — starlike planets — circle the sun between the orbits of Mars and Jupiter. They are only a few miles across, but show up on a photographic plate exposed for several hours as small stripes against the fixed points of the stars. In this way their positions may be plotted on maps. Saturn has three flat rings which encircle it, one band inside the other. Beyond the rings are nine moons. Uranus, Neptune, and Pluto are the remaining planets.

Other traveling bodies in space are *meteors* and *comets*. Meteors or "shooting stars" are ordinarily small particles that usually burn up when they strike the earth's atmosphere. Millions come into the atmosphere every day, but rarely penetrate it and reach the ground. The American Meteor Society has simple charts of the sky upon which may be marked the direction and path of meteors observed. Meteors may be seen on nearly any clear night, especially after midnight. It is not uncommon to see a dozen in an hour. Comets are made up mostly of glowing dust and gas. When they pass near the sun, frozen gases in the comet's head vaporize and stream out for millions of miles. The most famous comet is Halley's comet.

It completes its long orbit through the solar system every seventy-six years.

Man-made planets also orbit in space. Satellites now orbit the sun, and probes are planned to orbit Venus and Mars and attempt to take pictures. Maps will be made from these pictures and used by the first space explorers.

Of all the planets, Mars is the most clearly seen. It is not obscured by heavy clouds as is Venus, so it can be studied more carefully through our telescopes. Telescopic photographs show polar caps which enlarge and shrink in summer and winter. As the icecaps shrink, the green areas, which are thought to be vegetation, enlarge. There are no high mountains on Mars. Over one-half is smooth desert of reddish sand.

Mars has been more carefully mapped than any other planet except for Earth. For years many astronomers have seen a system of straight lines on Mars which appear to be huge man-made ditches or canals. Many made maps of what they saw. Now most astronomers think these are natural markings which only seem to be connected.

Unmanned missiles will perhaps soon circle Mars with television cameras to give us the answers to this and many other perplexing problems.

Perhaps in the future satellite observation will even reveal the existence of other worlds beyond our solar system! You may be sure if they do that the first steps will be to photograph and map them.

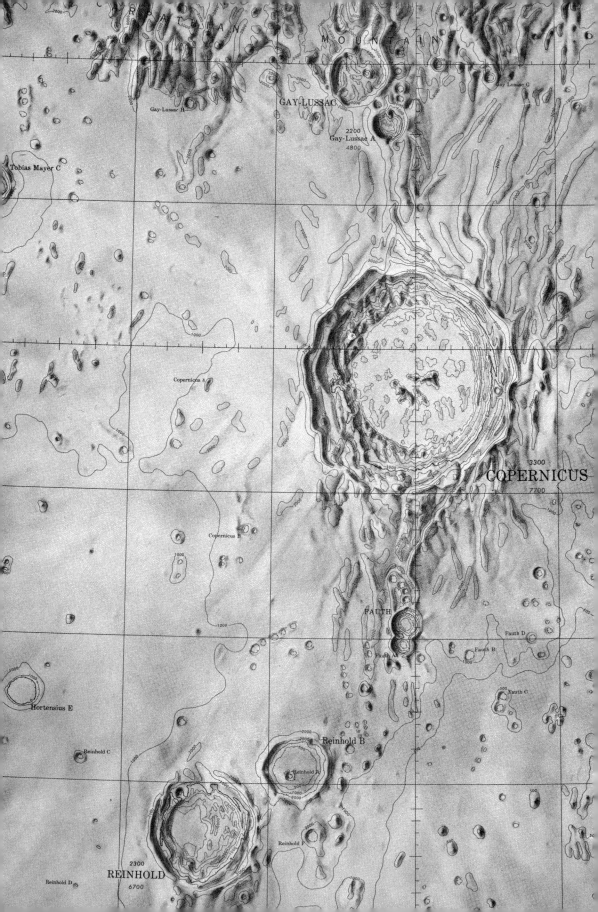

CARPATHIAN MOUNTAINS

GAY-LUSSAC

Gay-Lussac H

Gay-Lussac G

Tobias Mayer C

2200
Gay-Lussac A
4800

COPERNICUS

3300
7700

Copernicus 3

Copernicus B

FAUTH

Fauth D

Fauth B

Fauth A

Fauth C

Hortensius E

Reinhold B

Reinhold C

Reinhold A

REINHOLD

Reinhold F

2300
6700

Reinhold D

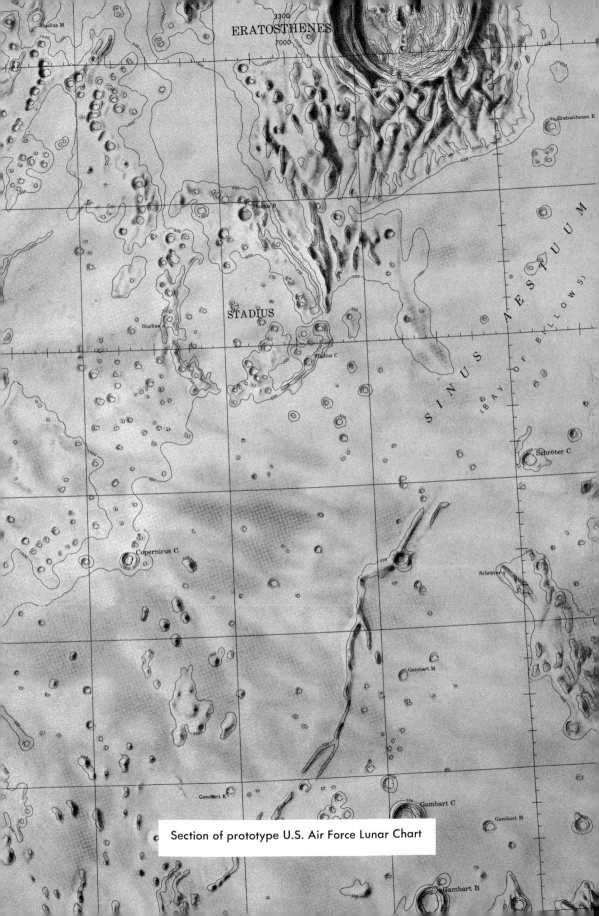

Section of prototype U.S. Air Force Lunar Chart

Map List

A list of some attractive, useful and inexpensive maps available.

MAP SERIES

Topographic Maps of the United States
> Contours, Wooded Areas, Roads, City and Town Areas. Colored. Size: 24x34 inches. Scale: 1:250,000. Other National Topographic maps are available from 1:24,000 to 1:1,000,000. Price: 50 cents. U. S. Geological Survey, Washington 25, D. C.

Nautical Charts
> Average size about 35x45 inches. Scale: from 1:2,500 to 1:1,200,-000. Price: from 25 cents to $1.00. U. S. Coast and Geodetic Survey, Department of Commerce, Washington 25, D. C.

Great Lakes Maps
> Average size: 30x38 inches. Scale: from 1:2,500 to 1:1,200,000. Price: $1.00. U. S. Army Engineer District, Lake Survey, Corps of Engineers, 630 Federal Building, Detroit 26, Michigan.

State Maps
> Base Maps, some with shaded relief, Contours and Highway Overprint. Not all states available. Various sizes. Scale: 1:500,000 and 1:1,000,000. Price: 25 cents to $1.00. Distribution Section, U. S. Geological Survey, Washington 25, D. C.

City Area Maps
> Cities and adjacent areas, Contours, Wooded Areas, Highways.

Average size: 42x58 inches. Scale: 1:24,000. Price: 20 cents to $3.00. U. S. Geological Survey, Washington 25, D. C.

National Geographic Maps

Detailed maps, many place names, all areas of the world. Colored. Size: 19x24¾ inches. Various scales. Seven maps per year with *National Geographic* magazine subscription. Price: 50 cents per map. National Geographic Society, Washington 6, D. C.

USAF Global Navigation and Planning Charts

Thirteen charts cover northern hemisphere, show relief, elevations, aerodromes, pattern of runways on larger airports, boundaries, railroads, highways and cities. Marked off in a one degree grid. Size: 41½x57½ inches. Scale: 1:500,000. Price: 40 cents. Aeronautical Chart and Information Center, Air Photographic and Charting Service, U. S. Air Force, St. Louis 18, Missouri.

Army Map Service Series—Europe, Southeast Asia, North Africa and Pacific Areas

Relief roads and cities. Colored. Various sizes (large). Scale: 1:6,336,000. Price: five sheets in series @ $1.00 each. Commanding Officer, Army Map Service, 6500 Brooks Lane N. W., Washington 25, D. C., Att: Map Distribution Division.

Landform Maps

United States and other areas of the world, carefully and accurately drawn, detailed maps of hills, plateaus, mountains, etc., with many place names. United States map size: 27x42. Price: 75 cents. Erwin Raisz, Cambridge 40, Massachusetts.

Plastic Relief Maps

Series covering the United States, showing populated places, roads, railroads, contours and woodlands. Colored. Scale: 1:250,000. Price: $4.00 per sheet. Commanding Officer, Army Map Service, 6500 Brooks Lane, N. W., Washington 25, D. C., Att: Map Distribution Division.

U. S. Daily Weather Map

Large weather map of the United States, showing individual weather stations. Smaller maps show yesterday's weather, high level contours, highest and lowest temperatures of weather stations across the United States, precipitation areas and amounts. Size: 19x24 inches. Price: 80 cents per month (no mailing charge). Superintendent of Documents, Government Printing Office, Washington 25, D. C.

MAPS OF SPECIAL INTEREST

Map of the World
> Easy-to-read map of the world. Colored. Size: 35x57 inches. Scale: 1:30,000,000. Price: $1.00. Amcrican Geographic Society, Broadway at 156th Street, New York 32, N. Y.

Physical-Political Global Chart of the World
> Colored. Size: 108x126 inches, issued in six sheets. Price: $2.10. U. S. Coast and Geodetic Survey, Department of Commerce, Washington 25, D. C.

Wall Map of the United States and Territories
> Shows national parks, Indian reservations, wildlife refuges, towns and railroads. Size: 5x7 feet, issued in two sheets. Price: $4.00. Superintendent of Documents, Government Printing Office, Washington 25, D. C.

Alaska Map E
> Excellent detailed relief map, showing cities, highways and glaciers. Colored. Size: 33x50 inches. Scale: 1:2,500,000. Price: 75 cents. U. S. Geological Survey, Washington 25, D. C.

Hawaii
> Separate maps of main islands. Colored. Scale: 1:250,000. Price: 50 cents each. U. S. Geological Survey, Washington 25, D. C.

Alluvial Valley of the Mississippi River
> Attractive map, showing levees, swamp areas, roads and timber areas. Colored. Size: 31x40 inches. Scale: 1:500,000. Price: 25 cents. Mississippi River Commission, Corps of Engineers, U. S. Army, P. O. Box 80, Vicksburg, Mississippi.

Topographic Map of Niagara Falls
> Streets, buildings, rapids and falls, with contours at 10-foot intervals. Colored. Size: 22x49 inches. Scale: 1:12,000. U. S. Geological Survey, Washington 25, D. C.

Yosemite Valley
> One of the finest of a series of shaded relief maps, with contour interval of 50 feet. Colored. Size: 18x36 inches. Scale: 1:24,000. U. S. Geological Survey, Washington 25, D. C.

Index

126

127